Advance Praise foı

"Daring, funny, candid, tender, *Bent But Not Broken* reveals the paradoxical truth about manhood: our strength as men is our weakness, and vice versa. Don Cummings is a witty, insightful writer, and this book is a marvel."

—John Sedgwick, author of *In My Blood: Six Generations of Madness and Desire in an American Family*

"*Bent But Not Broken* is a hilarious and deeply moving memoir about a penis and its owner. But more than that it's about the nature of love, the flux of relationships, and how bodies betray us all. Cummings is a stunning writer and excellent travel guide for this journey through his life."

—Maggie Rowe, Author of *Sin Bravely* and writer on *Arrested Development*

"Like his penis, Cummings gets bent out of shape, and not only on account of his condition: also just by being human, a man, a gay man who wants what he wants, as most of us do: love, intimacy, sex, money, fame, and sex. Cummings can't help but be funny, but he also can't stop being honest, and his writing achieves real poignancy that will grab you by the heart and penetrate deep into your soul, if you're the soulful type. If not, your mind, and definitely your memory. It's an unforgettable, beautiful book."

—Rick Whitaker, Author of *Assuming the Position* and *An Honest Ghost*

BENT BUT NOT BROKEN

BENT BUT NOT BROKEN

A Memoir

Don Cummings

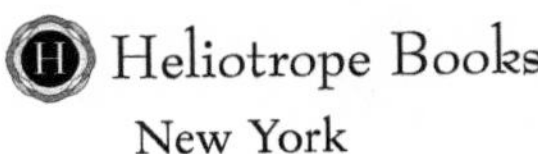

Heliotrope Books
New York

ISBN: 978-1-942762-61-4

Cover design by Chip Kidd
Interior by Naomi Rosenblatt

For Adam

The green reed which bends in the wind is stronger than the mighty oak which breaks in a storm.

—Confucius, and others

CONTENTS

·1·

THE ORIGINAL SIN

Men Are from Penis

I thought it might go away on its own. I had been having painful nighttime erections for six weeks. There was a grabbing sensation, an extra pressure just below the head on the right side of my penis. Sometimes the pain was mixed with more than the usual erectile pleasure because of the extra tightening, but only at half-staff. At first, I thought it was a good sign. My erections felt much stiffer than they had been our last few years in Los Angeles and our most recent year, in New York City. I thought it could be possible that my midlife hormone levels were on the rise. That was early February. By March, my tube steak, which had always been sizzling straight during erections, bent to the right about twenty degrees just below the glans whenever I came to attention. When my erection was at full capacity, it hurt. It was a piercing pain. I took pictures.

My boyfriend of sixteen years, Adam, and I had sex, but it was painful and difficult. It required contortions. One night early on, after he got home from work, I showed him one of the pictures.

"Look at this," I said.

"What is it?"

"My penis is not getting any better. It hurts almost all the time now."

He smiled, slightly supportively, somewhat derisively, as he always did when presented with any frailty, especially my frailties, which I made known at a moderate pace. Adam has an angelic sweetness mixed with a cool distance, like so many angels. The love, in its unique form, no matter the behavior, had always been there.

Before this discovery, we had been having great sex, having recently marooned ourselves in the borough of Queens, New York in our very inexpensive, three hundred and sixty-eight square foot studio apartment. Adam was in a career transition from television writing to digital marketing for a major cable network. I had followed my playwriting career, which was gang-busting, to New York. The most talented actress on earth, the one who once had serious dingo problems, performed a reading of my play at The Public Theater. A heady experience for sure, watching this genius act the antagonist of my life story as my loving but complicated mother. This character is on all sorts of pills, mostly painkillers, but she turns out to be the hero, the savior of a baby that is failing to thrive. Addiction and children and movie stars—I was guaranteed enormous success.

With few friends around and a tight, recession-proof budget, we were excited that we had the good sense to rent out the yellow 1924 bungalow we owned in Hollywood so we could be free and easy in our tiny Queens apartment during the worst financial disaster we had ever witnessed in the United States of America, land of endless opportunity. The used but new-to-us olive-green leatherette ottoman, practically stolen from our friend's house during an Oscar party in Mar Vista, right off the 405, for sixty-five dollars, then shipped to New York to become our foot rest and coffee table, was at a great height for most of our sexual menu choices. Being in such close quarters in Queens, "the sports and transportation borough," had made us more horny than cranky. Still attracted to each other, we enjoyed ourselves. Adam is blond and wispy and I am brown-haired and muscled. He is two inches taller. I am twenty pounds heavier. We are the same age, with midlife paunches. As for our worst personality traits, I am more volatile and he is more passive-aggressive. Neither one of us is entirely crazy. Our temperaments are nothing alike—if he's the bottom, I'm the top.

I pushed the picture closer to his face.

"I used your hand cream. Ignore the greasy white stripes and look at that bend."

"It's bent."

"Yeah. It's upsetting. It isn't getting any better."

He patted me on the shoulder.

"I hate when you pat me. Don't pat me." This had been going on for years.

"Sorry."

Adam pulled his hand far away from hostile territory. Automatically, I lifted my chin toward him, the worry expanding all the musculature around my eyes and forehead. Sadness drooped my lower lip, and my small jowls had no life in them. Something here from Boobsie? I waited. Then my whole face fell, and like I had during a million other moments of invisibility, I walked away to do some stupid chore, like finally picking up that dropped staple that had been sticking into my bare calloused heel whenever I walked on it. My colon tightened. Softness, with a craving for closeness, was replaced by resentment. I could have ripped up my used desk from a Palm Springs thrift store into well-varnished kindling and then lit the whole thing on fire. An older man with a reliable car who I briefly dated in college warned me years ago that affection and homosexuality were a tough mix.

Adam does not like to face problems head on. I face every problem like it will never go away. I had a feeling I would be on my own to solve this, as Adam would not even give visitors from Europe directions into town from the airport. He always said, "They're smart. They'll figure it out."

"Really? All the way from Gothenburg and you give them nothing?"

I have always been drawn to distant men. My father was a thin, pale, shy child of a drunk who learned early to disappear.

My mother was pregnant again a few days after I was born so she was preoccupied—with that and other things. I like people who don't care too much about me at first glance. I'm used to it. But I also hate it.

The sex with Adam had truly been great for the last few months and this made us feel closer. As some wise Italians repeat, "It is more important to have someone to hate than someone to love," and we had done our years of hatred, which kept the spark alive. We were reliant upon each other during this time of transition in Jackson Heights, Queens. But my erectile display threw us a curve and I grew anxious about abandonment. I had always used my penis as a connector. What if I lost this ability? If my penis were to cease to function, would I have regrets about how I had used it? Did I give Adam the best sex of his life? Did I give pleasure to enough other people along the way? Was my penis pressed into service too little? Was I being punished for having overused it?

By the third week, the pain at night was getting much worse. It woke me up. The pleasure of the extra pressure was completely gone, leaving me with nothing but vise-grip pain. I did not take any more pictures of my penis in its erect state. It was too difficult to manage the masturbation cream followed by the quick snapping with the camera—I did not want to mess up my cute aqua-faced Canon Powershot. I like to preserve things. My shirts last over ten years because I won't put them in the dryer.

I had always had a fear of Peyronie's disease. I had slept with men with curved penises and I had looked, long ago, into what could be the source. Being an undergraduate biology major, a pre-medical student, a curious sort, and fearful of deformities, I reached into my memory for a fast diagnosis. I had always been happy about the shape of my average-sized rocket. Not extra-long, but definitely thick—a 6 × 5, to be precise (the five being the circumference, not the diameter). I had been a welcome addition to many wanting dark spaces over the years. My Adam, legs over his head, never complained. He loved a sweet pounding. As I plowed through the field of life with its fecund and fallow seasons, I had at least had this decent tuber to hold on to. But blight was setting in, famine most likely soon to follow. Death felt more real. I was concerned that depression would take me over. It did—but not for long. His sharper cousin, anxiety, grabbed the wheel of the tractor. I had work to do.

What is the cause of this Peyronie's disease? I began to Google, like you do but shouldn't when you need answers to calm yourself down. Peyronie's disease is scar tissue, or plaque, made of naturally occurring fibrin that builds up in a disadvantageous location. It sandwiches between the outer layer of the two parallel dorsal (top) erectile tubes—remembered to me in Tufts pre-medical college classes as the Corpora Cavernosa—and the outer, reptilian, plate-like coating called the Tunica Albuginea, something I had never heard of before. This was interesting news to me—that there are these movable scales right underneath the penis skin, which expand and contract with the filling and draining of blood. The plaque can also build up underneath the single tube, the Corpus Spongiosum, which runs ventrally (underneath) and surrounds and protects most of the urethra—but this is less common. My buildup was surely on top. Every site gave the same explanation of how Peyronie's disease gets you: when your erection tubes, these Corpora Cavernosa, fill up with blood and there is obstructing scar tissue in the outer Tunica Albuginea, your penis bends in that direction. The plaque can eventually calcify. A solidified, wretched boomerang was possibly what I had to look forward to.

Fresh hell. —Remain calm. You can do this. Don't drive your man crazy with fear. He's at work. Figure it out. He scares easily.

I continued to read. Peyronie's disease, depending upon its severity, can lead to complete sexual dysfunction, with its visiting companions hopelessness, anxiety and depression. Peyronie's disease is most common in white, middle-aged men, especially men of Northern European heritage, so there is a genetic component. It is related to another condition, Dupuytren's contracture, a similar disorder in which scar tissue builds up at the inside base of fingers, which causes them to bend toward the palm of the hand, especially affecting the ring and smallest fingers. Peyronie's disease can be caused by an injury sustained while engaging in rough sex, especially if the penis is sharply bent at an angle, acute or obtuse. The thought and sound of that made me think back to the one time I had eaten jellyfish soup. The cool sliced body parts of that tasteless coelenterate between my teeth made a hard, crunching sound I felt as much as heard. Finally, I read that Peyronie's disease might be the result of an inflammatory auto-immune response and that alcohol only makes things worse.

I was perfectly positioned to have my penis repositioned into a painful bend. I was over forty-five years old upon discovery. My father is Scots-Irish-American with some German and Scandinavian thrown in. His father had Dupuytren's contracture of his right ring finger, but because he was a comedic alcoholic he had always told us grandchildren that his funky finger was from a wound he had sustained during World War I—that the doctors at that time couldn't do anything but sew his finger into that position. I had had rough sex with someone a few times over a period of a few months when Adam was still in Los Angeles packing up our house—I was lonely and needy in New York waiting for his arrival—but I had never heard the crunching jellyfish sound. Though I did use my member vigorously in and around this Broadway dancer guy who lived down the street, there was not much resistance and, truly, no pain on my part. In fact, the only thing that really hurt were my hands because he liked his ass to be slapped so hard. Though I felt mildly guilty about the sex—because even though Adam let me prowl, I am still culturally if not religiously Catholic—I did not think this new and rough action caused my new and rough reality. But who knew?

I was also kicked squarely in my plaid groin in the seventh grade. This scuffed the tip of my penis. The kicker was an eighth-grade girl who had colored the front strands of her hair bright green for St. Patrick's Day. When I asked her, "Hey Paula, what'd you do? Blow your nose in your hair?" she promptly went at my crotch with her mad work boot, sending me to the nurse's office and then home to see a doctor for the bleeding head that had scraped all along my zippered fly. I was not erect and was very young when this happened so that was probably not the cause. I have terrible allergies and get inflamed at almost everything. We had just endured this two-tiered move, me followed by Adam, across our economically-recessed country, with Adam thankfully changing careers and my writing projects all up in the air, being scrutinized for marketability, so I was drinking like a sailor.

The wise portion of my brain accepted that my dirty DNA was simply on the make, but also lurking was the self-punishing/delusional-controller part of me that believes I cause all the bad things that come into my life. I beat myself up thinking I willed this thing to happen by an accretion of shoddy actions, overuse, and roughness, including choosing to be born with less-than-perfect nucleic acids, the molecules that make up our DNA. Plus, in the 1980s, everyone I knew was a poor artist. We all read too many self-help books that told us we were the creators of our own realities. I hated that I had to take care of a new negative. I hated how it hurt all the time, now. I hated how it looked. The vain joke is, I had always wanted to be phenotypically expressed in the lighter, half-Irish mode over the thicker, darker half-Italian chunkiness that is the true cast of my face, brought upon me by my mother's side of the family. And now the wish had been granted, but in the wrong spot—a case of the Celtic tiger growling between my legs.

Adam was more supportive than I had hoped for but also self-protective and distant, like he did not want to be associated with something so terrible. He was tender with me after I finished having sex with him—first on the convenient ottoman and then on the edge of the bed, me standing. When I asked, "Was that okay? Did it feel okay? Is it real ugly?"

He said, "It's fine. It's fine."

When we had sex, I had to straddle one of his legs and move him to one side to slide my head into his anus. It was sex and it felt good but it also hurt, especially just before orgasm when my penis was at its hardest. In early sessions, Adam said he barely noticed it—but he was being nice and is a very untalented liar. When he glanced at one of my sideways-curved erections he got a look in his eye like someone who had just seen a two-headed mouse. I was getting more and more uptight and needed to fix this thing. I developed what felt like a bladder infection, that constant need to urinate, and a general burning sensation around the head of my penis, deep through my taint right up into my anus, like a hot brick had been dumped in what would be my uterus if I had one.

I began to think I had so much more wrong with me.

When I was eleven years old and my penis was still perfect, child-sized and not yet orgasmic, we moved five miles, from a white high ranch house in Spring Valley, New York to a hideous, three-story saltbox house in Suffern. The saltbox was built in the 1970s, the front of the lowest floor faced in barely-fired red bricks, some of them chalky white, the upper floors in cedar shakes, with the sides and back clad in light, butter-yellow shingles. It was on a corner lot and my mother swept the streets all around it every few weeks. She wanted something beautiful. What we had was something financially solid in a good school district. But no mistake could be made—our neighborhood was in the blue-collar section, scrappy and townie, near the ball fields with the summer carnivals, the water treatment works, the Ford plant, a dog food factory, a brake shoe manufacturer and Avon. The sound of freight trains slamming into each other at night as they coupled together, loaded with Fords for points north, south and west, was our lullaby. At Christmas season, our high school choir sang for the factory workers at Avon. I remember well the lipstick conveyer belt. I shared a bedroom with my brother. We had orange-and-brown striped, wall-to-wall shag carpeting. We picked it out.

We rented out the apartment on the very top floor, identical to our top floor except that it had a little balcony. If I was home sick from school I would go out our front door, take a three-foot walk to the door next to ours, climb the straight stairs, and visit the fun lady tenant, a mother of two, the same age as my mother. She was loud and alive, Mrs. Franzer. Like my mother, she worked at a doctor's office, but different hours, and wore a sort of white nurse outfit. And like my mother, she was an urban New Yorker—short, feisty, caring and a bit of a showgirl. It was easy to experience her as a surrogate parent on a sick Wednesday in February. I liked her, she liked me. We were both improvisational and enjoyed making things. She painted animal pictures and made flower arrangements. Her greatest work was a two-dimensional rooster made from an assortment of dried beans of different colors, shellacked for preservation. She could sew, too. She helped me understand how to make hand puppets.

In my sick child mind, I hated to suffer and wanted out. But what was the way out? How could a person stop suffering? Could a deal be struck? I was a wanting boy and pretended my thoughts were super powerful. I gave myself an ethical question to ponder. I felt guilty because it arose from a dark impulse. If I had a choice between being sick forever and Mrs. Franzer having to die, which would I choose? I imagined how awkward it would be to be super healthy while Mrs. Franzer had become a corpse and how guilty I would feel if that were to happen by my secret wishing. I was not a beast like Damien in *The Omen*. I knew I would have to choose being sick forever over her death, but I also knew it would be a very long and awful haul to be sick for eternity.

No endless pain for me, please. I continued to devour information online—the Peyronie's disease forums, institutes, chat rooms, the P.D. Wiki and other medical and historical sites about Peyronie's disease. There was one man's name that kept showing up on all the sites: Dr. Hellman (no real names of private citizens, except for Adam and me). For or against him, all these comments were a great advertisement. I looked up his website. He was, at the time, associated with the Sloan-Kettering urology department and was one of the premier Peyronie's doctors in the country, and this being New York City and me being parochial in that annoying Big Apple way, I figured he was probably the best on earth. Clearly he was the guy I had to call, since my pain and my curve were only getting worse. I could not do this on my own by obsessing online. Action, with the assistance of a trained professional, was what my pained penis needed.

I had to wait two weeks to make an appointment because we were switching our insurance from a COBRA situation, which, thank expensive-goodness, had been available to us after Adam was let go from Hollywood's stable of working television writers who were over forty, to employer-paid almost-free healthcare covered by Adam's temp agency. In the meantime, based on my online research (and do not take notes yet), I started to take extra vitamin E and bought Acetyl L-Carnitine for improved circulation and Neprinol, a scar tissue eater. These last two made me speedy, fuzzy and shaky, but until I could see the doctor there was not much else I could do. I tried to keep it light. I told Adam, "I've named my scar tissue Roberta Plaque."

"All your references are from the Seventies," he said.

This is often true.

We continued to have sex, but it became necessary to mostly stick with hands and mouths. It was very difficult to get the correct angle for anal insertion. Plus, I could end up puncturing a kidney with my right hook. Adam loved me being top man. Now, I was the underdog. I wondered if he would be able to survive in this relationship without getting what he mostly liked. Or if I could face being the source of his and my daily disappointment.

Patience. Breathe.

·2·

PROFESSIONAL OPINION

It's a Stretch

After two weeks, I went in to see Dr. Hellman. I had to check in at the desk in the street-level lobby of a nice building on a brownstone street in the East Sixties. Tony neighborhood for a midlife penis problem. The officious man at the desk, young and shut down, someone I could have easily become since I am good with paperwork and orderliness, took all my information. I tried to be friendly, looking for a human connection, compassionate that he was stuck in an administrative job that was most likely a monstrous bore. I smiled and chatted and fluttered. He remained professional and uninterested. Here I was, finally at the entrance to Dr. Hellman's altar, and the guard would not celebrate my arrival. I was concerned that Adam's new temp agency health insurance would not work because I am concerned that most things in our country do not work. The desk man looked it up and told me, "We are in contract with them." His *froideur* made me nervous, which always shuts down my comprehension as my cognition scrambles with anxiety. I did not understand exactly what *in contract with them* meant.

"Do you take this insurance?" I asked.

"Yes, we are in contract with them," he said coldly, emphatically, again.

"So that means you take this insurance?"

"Yes."

—Goodbye, jerk. I mean, really. I have a curved penis that no longer works properly and I am so happy to finally *be* here at Sloan Kettering to get this taken care of and you stick to the script? In contract could mean almost anything. I've never heard that before. Okay. I'm ramped up. In contract. In contract. I'll let this poor guy go about his day. I'll just head down the elevator. It's not his fault I feel lonely and vulnerable, unattractive and unwanted. Time, that nasty fourth dimension, did what it did to me.

Back when we were living with Reagonomics, I was the guy who would walk into my college cafeteria strategically exposing a freshly worked out chest in a ripped, maroon, medium weight, double weave, loose-fitting T-shirt that was a little too short—okay, girly—and hung above my belt line that said, in white, embossed, hard, cotton letters: *Impale Yale, Harvard-Yale, the Gam*e, in a grungy swipe at the Ivy League. This well-traveled, floppy shirt was aspirational—I was attending neither Harvard, down the street, nor Yale—but more importantly, it was sexually strategic. Because it was ripped at one armpit and just below the opposite nipple, and because of its lacking length, showing a decent section of my navel love trail, it telegraphed the ironic tone that I had actually been mauled in a football game, impaled, something an arty annoyance like me would have never experienced unless there was a lot of alcohol and porn involved. It flaunted that I was proud to be from a lower class than most of these precious egg-munching toffs on this side of the Medford, Massachusetts hill. If anyone had any objection to my trashy getup, I was never told about it.

We all just had to face it—Yale and Harvard only existed so this T-shirt could be made, worn into soft attraction, lost by someone unknown, found or stolen by me in the laundry room, and then donned so I could look good walking down the steps into MacPhie Dining Hall, with my meal card and my bouncing confidence. I enjoyed the adrenaline and serotonin rush as I watched the coeds and the interested boys pretend they were not tilting their heads upward toward the *Brady Bunch* slatted stairway to surreptitiously stare at my fat-free abs and heaving, hard tits. It was a tacky move, but like my lively mother, I knew how to get attention. Mousey as a boy and anything-but later on, with loose gold and auburn curls down to my shoulder framing the intact, chiseled skull of my energized late-adolescence, I pretty much wanted to go fuck myself.

Leaving the desk man behind, now that we were in contract, I crossed to the elevator and hit the C for Concourse, which was really the basement of the building—but nicely, it was an atrium, since the ceiling had a huge cutout to the first floor above. Lots of natural light. Magazines. Almost like a college student center with its blond wood. But I was not a student now. I was a weird grown man, not so sexy, in a large waiting room, surrounded by mostly older men with their caring wives. I thought how nice it would be one day, when Adam and I were old, to go to doctor's appointments together. Until then, I would soldier on, in this basement aerie, and get this penis fixed. Alone. I could do it.

I emailed Adam.

Nice waiting room.

Pause.

I don't know how long I'll have to wait.

Pause.

—He's busy, he's busy. Thank God he got this gig. Damn recession. Okay.

The insurance worked. I was so grateful that Adam was toiling and we were safe from financial ruin. How do single people live? How can you face the horror of decay and ruin all alone? Like a housewife in a black-and-white sitcom, nailing down security has always been my essential motivation. When this is in full force I can push against it in controlled rebellion and really enjoy the day. —Thank the ever-loving savior for working boyfriends.

Thank you, God, who I don't even know at all, for the energy of possibility. This is bigger than my atheist self.

I went in to speak to this upbeat man, this Dr. Hellman, about a quick look-see at my penis-horrible. He resembled the actor who played Murray on *The Mary Tyler Moore Show*, Gavin MacLeod. He had very good, clipped diction.

"Hello."

"Hi."

"When did you start to notice the bending?"

"Two months ago."

"Is there pain?"

"Yes."

"On a scale of one to ten, how strong is the pain?"

"Oh, just a two or three, but it never really goes away."

"We do not know what causes Peyronie's disease. We believe there is a genetic component. Your name is Cummings, so I assume Northern European ancestry?"

"My father, yes. Irish, some Scottish and German ..."

"You see, it runs in families."

"My grandfather had a completely bent ring finger."

Dr. Hellman did not show that he cared that my grandfather had a bent finger.

Dr. Hellman told me what he must have told so many upset men before me. He remained upbeat and compassionate. He spoke quickly, in the way you do when you have to say something you've already said a thousand times. He did not talk down to me, though. I was all ears, all attention.

"Some think it might be caused by a virus, but we have not been able to find a virus. Some say it can be caused by injury, but most people who come in here do not remember being injured. It's genetic. We really believe it is genetic."

"Great."

"How much is it bending? And where is it? Show me."

With that, he handed over a four-inch, skinny rubber dildo in the shape (and with the veiny-ness) of a penis. Perhaps he presented such a small phallus so no one would feel less-than or intimidated? I showed him the spot where it was bent. He asked me, "How much does it bend?"

"About like this." I pulled the rubber penis head to the right about twenty-two degrees.

He asked me, "Can you still have sex?"

"It bends to the right at the top, not too much, but enough so that I have to maneuver in order to get it correctly input. But it hurts. So sort of. Not really. We're not having much sex right now."

"How are your erections?"

"My erections are strong."

"That's good."

—Great.

"And you came in early. Most men wait to come in until it's too late. Most gay men come in sooner than straight men since they are more identified with their penises."

—Well, there's an advantage to the gay thing, finally.

Dr. Hellman told me to go to the desk in the waiting area to set up an appointment for a curvature assessment. He explained that this would involve injecting my penis to bring it to a full erection so they could measure the curvature and also take an ultrasound to examine the shaft for plaque. If the test showed that I needed Verapamil injections—and I had a strong feeling the test would because he was in the Verapamil business—I would have to come in six times over a period of twelve weeks to be numbed and injected. He said, "Set up the six appointments so you'll be on the books because the schedule gets full, and if the assessment test shows that you do not need Verapamil injections, you can cancel them."

"Right."

I also had to make an appointment to have my blood drawn before arriving at any of these appointments, to measure my testosterone levels, so Dr. Hellman gave me a preapproval for a phlebotomist, a person who draws your blood. Dr. Hellman said, "I assume your testosterone is going to be fine, though. You are young."

"Okay. Are you going to examine my penis?"

"Yes, right now."

I dropped my drawers. He felt around, probing for nodules.

—Go for it, Dr. Hellman.

"Yes, I do feel something. It will be good to look. Okay. Good. Now I'm going to stretch it. Are you ready?"

Dr. Hellman took the tip of my penis, just about a centimeter at the end, between his thumb and his pointer finger and stretched it about as long as I have ever seen it flaccid. It resembled what I have seen in a microscope lens of a planarian, a flatworm, the simplest bilateral animal. And then he let it go, not unlike a slingshot. He was confident. "You have a very good stretch. This is good. Okay. You can pull up your pants."

(You can cut a planarian bilaterally, horizontally, or vertically and it will grow into two worms. Or split its head and it will grow two new full heads on the same body. Cut it up into pieces, you will grow as many worms as pieces. Such worms!)

I pulled up my pants. I was glad I had a good stretch. A part of me thought—I'm always lucky. I am. This is going to work out. I always come out okay. Uh-huh.

Dr. Hellman assured me, "The good news is it only happens to you once in a lifetime. After a year or eighteen months the pain will go away. It always does."

I thought—But then you are left with a cruller between your legs?

I was very curious about the treatments that I would be having and eager to begin. I asked the doctor how they worked.

Dr. Hellman told me, "Think of a piece of scotch tape on a balloon. When you blow up the balloon it bends in the direction of the tape because of the constriction. We need to break up that tape."

Dr. Hellman explained the treatments. "You will be receiving a mixture of Verapamil, an off-label blood pressure medication, and saline. This will be injected into the hardening plaque. The sooner the better, to soften it before it becomes calcified. We do not know if it is the Verapamil, the saline or the needle that does the trick."

Frigging known unknowns.

Then he assured me, "In forty percent of patients, it gets better. Another forty percent, there is no change. In twenty percent, it gets worse. So you have an eighty percent chance that it will at least remain the same or get better."

He was pleased with these statistics, as if his life's work was not based on snake oil salesmanship or positive-thinking hoopla. A man of science and math. Great. I was with him. I hung onto those very good odds. On the other hand, I had to consider my mother who has been riddled by so many diseases that have never been improved by conventional medicine. Her baleful immune system has eaten away at her organs and tissues to such excruciating pain that she has had to endure her last few decades on earth on a phalanx of steadily prescribed Oxycodone. But was I only my mother's son? No. Maybe. No.

When I first called to make this appointment I was asked to bring any supplements that I was taking. I showed Dr. Hellman my booty bag. His seen-it-all-before face telegraphed that he was disappointed that I was so easily conned, that I had been spending too much time online with the charlatans. He pushed the multi-vitamins aside as if they were harmless and then held up the bottle of vitamin E. "The vitamin E won't hurt you, but we have seen no studies that prove it helps."

"Oh, okay. It's all over the internet."

"The Acetyl L-Carnitine won't hurt you, but again, any help might be negligible."

Then he picked up the Neprinol. "This ... is garbage."

"What should I do with it?"

"Throw it away."

Dr. Hellman warned me that people take advantage of this fraught situation to sell these useless supplements. On its official website, Neprinol is listed as a dietary supplement that contains a proprietary combination of enzymes and cofactors. It claims to keep your fibrin levels adjusted, naturally reducing any excess scar tissue in your body. Sounded good to me. Dr. Hellman loathed the stuff as a serious time and cash detour.

I was happy to be rid of these things, since I hated them all. Most drugs either speed me up or bring me down. The Acetyl L-Carnitine and the Neprinol supplements were of the speedy variety. No need for them. But what if Dr. Hellman was just another guy selling his own ideas for fun and profit? We do live in a land of sales first, empirical knowledge second, after all. But my gut sense, which of course could have been wrong, told me he was right. Plus, I like physical, cutting solutions to problems more than pills. If you can do something physical, like sinus surgery instead of endless decongestant pills, I say snip out the offending tissue! I'm ready!

I told Dr. Hellman I was also taking cranberry pills because, "I feel like I have a constant need to go to the bathroom. I must have a bladder infection. My prostate feels inflamed. I feel like something hot and terrible is happening in my groin and buttocks area, in general. Like it's all inflamed."

"You are over-concentrating on your penis. It is important that you do not do this. Everything else you have going on is in your mind. You may have what is called chronic pelvic pain syndrome. There is a drug for that."

"Really? What causes this?"

"It comes from adrenaline and being nervous. Are you a type A personality?"

"Of course I am."

"You just need to relax. When you get your blood work done I am sure they will find nothing. You are too young to have anything wrong with your prostate. You need to stop thinking about all of this and get on with regular things."

I thought back to the time in Los Angeles that I was convinced I had GERD. I was panicked about it and I did not want to take medication. I was shaking at the gastroenterologist's office on Beverly Boulevard, across from Mt. Sinai Hospital, a wreck about facing a lifetime of acid reflux and daily purple pills, when the wonderful Dr. Duoberg looked me right in the eye and hypnotized me with a positive suggestion, saying, "I don't believe you have GERD or acid reflux or anything like that. I just think you have sensitive body issues." Within three days I was cured. Now then, this Dr. Hellman in New York was onto something about me, how I somaticize my nervous energy. I understood this territory of my unconscious makeup and knew instinctually I could calm down my pelvic floor. Even thinking about it calming down calmed it down. But this bent penis? A flaw in my personality was not making this up.

Dr. Hellman handed me a brochure for the AndroPenis. This is a penis stretcher. Stretching is important for Peyronie's disease. He said I should order one. "I get nothing for suggesting this company. There are other ones out there, but this is the best one. Insurance does not cover it so you will have to spend the three hundred dollars, but it's worth it since it really does work."

"Okay." Money. Money. Money.

"You wear it four to six hours every day for six months, maybe longer. It lassos behind the head of the penis with two spring-action tension rods. The DVD that comes with it shows you how to do it. Every two weeks you add a half centimeter of length by screwing on extender disks. Much like the way some African tribes do their necks, your penis will lengthen and straighten. Follow the instructions."

Oh Christ. Now there's a chore. But I'll do it. For me. For Adam. For Africa. For everyone.

Before I left, he repeated something he had already told me twice, "Remember, no one ever died from Peyronie's disease."

I thought—Of course, no one knows the cause of every suicide.

·3·

THE CHALLENGE

Personal Dick-Sastor

I ordered the AndroPenis stretcher by phone. More difficult than takeout but a little easier than discount blinds, the man on the other end took my order and assured me it would arrive within five days. There were no choices to make. One kit with DVD instructions. I emailed Adam at work in Midtown Manhattan with the results of my appointment with Dr. Hellman by sending him a link to an article about the fun of future Verapamil-filled needles plunging into my penis.

Adam responded digitally.

Dear lord! I'm SOOOO sorry, honey! What a drag! But at least now you know you're not crazy. The shots don't sound like much fun. Don't worry, my darling, we'll get through this. Wrapping up here in a half hour, then off to gym then home to you and the clams.

Linguine with clam sauce was the first thing he ever made for me. It was always comforting. Such love.

I emailed back:

No, I'm not crazy…but all the pelvic discomfort I have is called Chronic Pelvic Pain Syndrome. It's a nervous thing. So that's a little crazy. I have to go back to meditating, baby. Heaven help me. But at least it isn't cancer—

That was Monday.

Two days later I left my apartment in Jackson Heights, Queens, drove to Astoria in our graphite Ford Focus with the alternator trouble, found easy parking, and went to the phlebotomist. A sunny day. Whenever I find free and easy parking I feel like someone is on my side. Then I entered. Every person working in the office was an African-American woman having a good time. Not to be racist, but I tend to love black women. Not as much as Adam does. He always wanted to *be* a black woman. I am more realistic about what can happen on earth. They had me fill out the usual forms. New software had been installed and no one was able to use it. The largest lady of them all read from the prescription to input into the system what they were to test for. She pushed some keys and simply could not make anything happen at all.

"I'm trying to pull up the code. I can't pull up the code. I don't know what's wrong with this machine." She turned to her easy-going chum. "Hey, how do I get this code in?"

"What is it?"

"Testosterone."

"Testosterone?"

"Yeah, testosterone. Hey, that's a hormone!"

They both cackled, then practically high fived. The idea of something being a hormone and then getting to say it out loud! Like in grade school, and mostly, I believe, because of the syllable "whore." Anything to break up their dull days. I understood dull days.

"Well, let me see."

The chum wheeled over and clicked a drop-down menu on the screen. They were both still alive with joy from their joke.

"That's the code. Right there."

"Oh, I got it. Thanks. Testosterone."

The largest one of all was happy about punching in the code. From her cocked head and her satisfied cheeks, it appeared like this was the first time she had ever succeeded with this brand new system. I was happy for her, but I stood there tight-lipped with disapproval over their locker-room behavior. I was ready for the two of them to get up and bump bellies. She felt my disdain and embarrassment and the full flush of her happiness drained.

I try to keep a kind poker face when things are awful but it was probably clear that I kind of wanted to kill them all. I went into a room. They drew my blood. I left.

They never called me with the results.

I never called to get them.

Walking back to my well-parked Ford, I thought of my privates from when I was a kid. They were fodder for public reaction then, too. But by my choice.

My penis would get erect for no reason. My brother, eleven months younger, had the same experience. As adults, the Early-Morning-Woody, or Piss-Boner, is something most men know well, until they don't. As a child, it was all newfound fun and games. It was the late 1960s so we called our penises in the erect state "rockets." As in, "Hey, Mom, look at my rocket." We did not show our mom frequently, but when we did, she would smartly laugh it off. My father, a wee Irish about it all, would get flustered but smile. Sometimes we would put on a show, run into the family room grabbing our testicles, one in each hand and sing, "COcoNUTS, bah, bah, BUM, COcoNUTS, bah, bah, BUM," and pull our balls up and down on each bah, bah, BUM, as if they were dancing to the tune. This tropical nut action was in good fun and was always presented without a rocket. A rocket would have eclipsed the testicle dance. The coconuts were always there, but a rocket was more special, like some sort of tool that could be used to point the way to something fun or to poke someone in the eye. Like Major Tony Nelson living in Cocoa Beach on *I Dream of Jeanie*, we may have loved our coconuts, the possibility of magic, but we loved our rockets more.

Friday. I went back to Dr. Hellman. He gave me a quick hello. I had my vitals taken by a staff member and it turned out that I had lost a good amount of weight. Six pounds. I was handed over into another room for my curvature assessment. A nurse practitioner, a solid female citizen from Park Slope, Brooklyn, walked in. She had strong dark hair and pale skin. She was in her thirties, bright-eyed and optimistic. She looked like she could be my cousin or a neighbor, a familiar face. Standing over her tray with the shot for erecting she said, "The needle is going to go in at two o'clock or at ten o'clock."

I did not understand what she meant. —How are those positions on a penis? Is this woman looking at a penis as if it is the face of a clock? From which direction? As if she is me, or as if she is a dog looking at my glans covered with shredded corned beef?

She swabbed the base of my penis with alcohol. The shot came quickly. Okay, it went in on the left side about a third of the way down, so two o'clock if you are looking at a cross section like a pooch staring up from a braided rug. It wasn't terrible, really, this shot. Plus, my physical pain tolerance has always been exceptionally high. I wish my mind were similar. My penis began to get chubby.

Ms. Slope handed me a manila envelope with pornographic magazines inside. Trying to be light about it, she took on a jokey tone about the porn, "Here you go! Get yourself ready!"

This felt dismissive and businesslike to me. Such poor, odd timing for levity. To be so intimately joshing and so distant at once got up my hackles, and being that she was a woman, this was not a turn-on. No offence to my XX sisters. Apparently, it was time to masturbate. I'd had no idea I would have to get the party going after the shot was administered, and there she was, this big lady lesbian, treating me like just another patient. I felt put upon. I felt mistreated. I felt humiliated. I was furious.

Apparently, adrenaline is the antidote to a good erection. After Ms. Slope gave me the first needle and left the room, yanking the curtain around me, I grew very nervous. I became a sweating machine on the examination table, with my bad copy of *Latin Inches*, trying to get a full erection. As I rubbed my penis head to get things going, trying to remain calm and focused, the thin medical onion-skin paper underneath me was sticking all over my wet ass and lower back. I was mad as hell, half muttering, while starting to jerk off—This is ridiculous. I can't believe they didn't tell me I would have to get myself up. I thought the shot alone would do it. I hate this. I just hate this. When are they coming back in? Okay, I'm ready now. It's up. Let's get this over with. Now. Where are you? Where are you people? Why don't they give you a buzzer to let them know you are ready for inspection? This is awful.

The first shot was not enough. As soon as she came in to check on me my raging penis flopped down like a dead seal flipper. The nurse practitioner administered a second shot, this time quietly and with more concern. She left. That second dose did the trick. Nothing could stop it. I could have been looking at naked pictures of my great grandmother and I would have remained erect.

My tumescent penis was huge and hard. Okay, six inches long and very thick, like we liked it. It had not been this erect since the problems began. Now I could see exactly the shape of the deformity in its full proportion. At the bottom, it was lumpy and thick like a sweet potato, sort of squatter than I remembered. But this may have been an optical illusion caused by the geometry of the neighboring shape because at the top it resembled a side-leaning fiddlehead fern. There are no recipes for this sort of monster.

I perseverated.

—In what universe will this thing ever be useful? Will I need an alien species to adopt me? What on earth caused this other-worldly troll between my wet, sweating thighs? How did this happen to me? Did I cause it by using that cheap vacuum pump a few times back in the '90s? Or maybe it *was* from the Paula cock kick in junior high, or surely from those times I bedded down with the masochistic Broadway dancer down the street in Queens and I kept slapping his face with my penis, hard, because he wanted it rough, and I didn't even want to do it at all, really, I just wanted love, I'm so codependent—or maybe, like the title of that book I never read claims, it was just the result of a general condition that can be found in that catch-all bowl, *When Bad Things Happen to Good People*, even though none of us really know exactly what good people are. It was hard. This was hard.

A new urologist, Dr. Scavone, came in to do the ultrasound.

A smallish man, clearly harboring repressed anger, ill at ease, he covered my penis with a gel and went up and down the sides with the wand. No fetus in there. Certainly this was not being recorded for Facebook. He was looking to see if the plaque had become calcified yet, which would be a bad thing and actually impossible to treat without an operation. I was slab flesh to him. He was as distant as a star. I retreated deep into my skull, wishing for this thing to end. Far away, Dr. Scavone lay down the ultrasound hose and then pulled out a clear, plastic, grade school protractor. He set the zero point where the rightward-bending curve began. He asked about my present erection. "On a scale from one to ten, how would you rate your hardness?"

I said, "I can't really get into numbers right now."

"You have to."

"Okay. A nine." —Why not? I was not as hard as I had been a few minutes ago, but certainly hard enough to be a proud nine.

He marked down a few things. This was pretty quick, this assessment. He blinked a few times. Nothing more. His personality seemed ready-made for a Russian science fiction film, but with less warmth and cheer. He left. Goodbye, gray soul.

I waited a few minutes, looking at my distortion. The examination was over and I could let this potato-and-fern salad wilt. Minutes later, Dr. Hellman returned. He said, "Well, the good news is you have great blood flow." This meant that I was not at all impotent. Great. Then I blew up.

"You didn't tell me I was going to have to stimulate myself. I thought I was going to get a needle and that would be that. I am already having enough problems without the humiliation of having to get myself excited. And that nurse! She didn't even care. She was joking with me. Do what you want, but you have to explain everything to me from now on. Everything. Every single step. I don't want any more surprises."

Dr. Hellman was flustered but kept his cool with his crimson face and cherry-red skull. I was appreciative that he remained calm and I was embarrassed by my outburst. But I did mean it.

"We give you the magazines so we can give you as few shots

as possible. Adrenaline works against erections. You're a type A person. Now we have to wait until your erection comes down. You can't go home until that happens. It's not safe. You do have Peyronie's disease but it's mild. You should do the six treatments."

I cried.

"I know it's hard. You're probably the inserter, yes?"

"Yes."

"It's a slight case but it is in the worst spot, right below the head."

"I know."

"This makes it hard to insert because you need the head as a battering ram." He made a fist and held his wrist with the other hand as a visual aid. He didn't have to. I had been living the depletion.

"So you have what we call *wobbly head*. Go sit outside for fifteen minutes. If your erection does not go down that's dangerous and we'll have to give you another shot to reverse it."

I sat in the hallway. I was happy to know that he intuitively thought of me as a top. I am pretty tough and stocky and like being *male* in that old-fashioned pumping way.

After fifteen minutes my erection did not abate. Ms. Slope came up to me in the row of lavender-gray chairs where I was waiting and asked how I was doing. I grimaced and nodded my head a bit, indicating she should take a look at the state of my penis. She brought me back into the examination room. She was very calm and not at all jokey like she had been earlier. Dr. Hellman must have told her they had a real live one on their hands. She said, "I hear you're from California." She had lived there, too. She talked about adrenaline again but spoke warmly, with a comforting tone. I felt like she cared about me as she stuck a third needle into the side-center of my shaft, at about ten o'clock, to bring it down. "You might get dizzy." I did. She stood there, still and open. Receptive.

I said, "I'm sorry I blew up. I told the doctor you were cavalier and were joking around. This is really sensitive. I'm sorry. I'm upset."

She said, "I understand. It is sensitive."

She had me wait another ten minutes to make sure it was safe to release me. It was. I was completely deflated.

On my way out, I emailed Adam.

I have Peyronie's disease and though it is not terrible when it comes to degree...it is actually in the worst place that you can have it. Right below the head. So now I have what is called a wobbly head...But I INSIST on not getting depressed about it. This day was traumatic, humiliating and I Can't Believe It's Not Butter. Don

A few minutes later.

I just went into the bathroom and sobbed. I don't know whether to go home and come back or go home and not come back. You should probably call me right now. Don

Then—

OK, I am not going back to Queens. I am going to World Wide Plaza. Meet me there and we will go to David and Cynthia's together. I do not have the cava.

And another one.

Meet me at wwplaza.

And then another one after I got there.

I'm on the southeastern edge just outside of the Mother Burger patio.

·4·

SURE, GO HOME AGAIN

The Knack for Peyronie's

We had dinner with David and Cynthia, the couple who had introduced us to each other, from afar in New York, with the aid of a mutual friend in Los Angeles, so long ago. More dinners and regular days passed, the dull pain of the penis-crunching plaque never letting me forget that my first Verapamil injection was coming soon. I was grateful to be in the hands of a medical professional and for Adam's cheery, though cool, support. Positive in disposition, but hobbled by breeding, he was only effusive when he drank, and that could go either way. I was on the hunt for emotional support that was unmeasured, with the proper combination of *That-is-so-awful-you-poor-thing* and *You-are-going-to-heal-one-hundred-percent-because-I-love-you-and-I say-so*, unflagging. Obviously, I am not the quiet suffering type. I am more the verbal volcano trying to get people to agree with my delusion that the right combination of love and care will make it possible not to have to endure pain at all. And if I do have to suffer, because it is inevitable, it should all terminate in an anxiety-free ending. I think of all those people who have beautiful deaths surrounded by their loved ones. Everyone around them. Mom, dad, sister, brother, beagle.

The next weekend I was eating and smoking on the backyard deck of my brother Charlie's house in Mahwah, New Jersey—a small family gathering with his local in-laws. I approached my sister, Sarah, director of reimbursement in a large Bergen County, New Jersey hospital and a former X-ray technician. At first, I did not want to tell anyone in my family about my penis problem, but why not reach out for some backup? I am not often ashamed by my shortcomings or bad luck. However, in this area I was embarrassed while inwardly screaming for compassion and did not want my sister to experience me as a flailing man. Plus, her strategy for handling stress is often a big pull-in like my father, like Adam, like England, like America. I presented my affliction to my sister with concern for my brother. I told Sarah about the Peyronie's disease, explaining what it was, what the procedure was going to be. Then I asked, "Do you think I should tell Charlie? It's genetic. Should I warn him?"

In addition to looking for a sisterly buoy, I truly was concerned about the future waters of my brother's boating career. Sarah grew in strength. She gave me the *Doctors-know-what-they-are-doing-you-are-going-to-be-fine* energy, this from a woman who had had the mid-life cervix woes of the freezing and scraping of unwanted cells, like so many women have, like so many gay men have in their cloacae. It helped. I got the hit I needed. I should trust her more. I grew a little less anxious. Didn't working in the health industry in any way at all make her an expert on procedures? It certainly gave my mother permission to write drug prescriptions when she was a medical secretary. Medicine: the family business I did not go into but the group vacation I often sign up for.

With Sarah's flat endorsement of my okay future, I figured I would tell my brother, not for his view from the open-legged stance of the car salesman that he is, but more because I felt like he should be warned. My sister could maybe be supportive, and she was, even if a bit too calm, but my brother, he is a golfer and a fisherman and not prone to thinking too much about crappy things.

I have been protective of my little brother and I have always had the feeling that I could handle any God-given smites on earth, that if they were to be doled out and if there was to be a choice between us, I would be more equipped to handle them. Plus, he had been hit by a car in the third grade and broken so many major bones: skull, pelvis, ribs, vertebrae, my mother's heart, almost my parents' marriage, that he deserved no more misery. He almost died from that auto disaster on Union Road in Spring Valley, New York, but he rallied, temporarily cross-eyed, crooked-tongued and manic. This was a monstrous turning point for my family.

My father comes from a large clan, and within a twenty-four-hour window of my brother being mowed down by a speeding teenager, one of my uncles died, my father's favorite brother. No one from the Cummings side, grieving as they were, was equipped to take on the babysitting chores for my sister and me while my mother and father spent every hour at the hospital with my brother, who was in critical condition. This slight was the final straw on the back of my sensitive camel mother, who perceived it as yet another dismissal by my father's family, "those fucking useless Irish drunks," and it solidified our family into cohesion—and also my father's family of birth, who circled their caravans a safe distance from us—as my parents saved and slaved and kept us on a steady path through elementary school, moved us to a better town, Suffern, the one with the two-family house, and paid for our ski lessons, music lessons, pizza slices and the occasional vacation to an Atlantic beach. We made wonderful friends and never looked back at Spring Valley, the high ranch, the low point locus of our lives. We arrived in Suffern in time for puberty. Fun.

Charlie survived the accident with a lifetime of headaches and backaches. We are only eleven months apart and when we were both about twelve years old there was a lot of boy-on-boy action in our neighborhood. It was mostly playful and inquiring, but for me it was getting sexually enjoyable. So when Peter, a kid our age, would rub up against one of us as a joke or when Will and Tim played the game where you breathed in and out real fast sixty times to raise your carbon dioxide level and then had someone grab below your ribs and squeeze your diaphragm until you passed out, which would sometimes get followed up by a fun penis being put in your gaping unaware mouth, I noted that homosexuality was in the air and on my tongue, and I did not want my brother to have to face the sad life of a faggot. That's what we called a boy who liked to have sex with boys. He did not end up gay from those silly boy games where a penis was used as a toy for a practical joke. Though once, a mentally challenged man at the Black Bridge, our hangout near the Mahwah Ford Plant, approached my brother while fishing, penis flailing, saying, "Touch it, touch it." My mother taught my brother well. He ran home and told her immediately. The police found the penis exposer quickly and they put him away.

Now, as an adult with my compromised penis and my brother at a safe distance from speeding cars, homosexuality and fisherman predators, I wanted to make sure he would be safe from other wretched ills. I pulled him aside as homemade Mahwah, New Jersey wine and store-bought ice cream were going round and told him about my Peyronie's disease and its possible basis in DNA and what he should look out for. His eyes grew wide. He said, "Sorry, bro. I'm fine."

I had seen my brother's penis many times as a child. Pissing in the woods, in the toilet, in the snow, changing clothes. I cannot remember exactly what it looked like, but I do remember it was similar to mine. During my early adolescence, I was standing in the hallway of our house in Suffern near the stairs that shot down to the finished basement. The flooring was dark, shiny, deep brown and made from a solid piece of vinyl. It was designed to resemble knotty planks. It was so fake looking I always wondered why they even bothered trying. Somehow, the subject of my penis size came up with my mother as my feet stuck to the floor. I was showing some sort of vulnerability about growing up. I was concerned about my body. My mother and I were pretty close so it was natural to talk about these things, even though I sensed that putting some distance between us was probably a wise strategy for my teen years. We were both pretty volatile people. I was also feeling like my brother and I were growing apart, which upset me. My mother turned to me and said, "Maybe you're just upset because your brother's penis is larger than yours."

By my rigid posture, she immediately understood she was wading into delicate waters. My mother was always lively and pushed things to the edge, but she wasn't a complete maniac. To lighten things up, she went to grab at me, almost like a tickle. Just as I turned to get away from her, she grabbed my crotch. I do not think she was trying to grab my penis and balls. I assumed she was trying to grab my ass, to give me a funny goosing, and that I turned at the wrong time. On the other hand, I do remember it was such a solid grab I wondered if it could have been anything but premeditated. I was aghast. She recoiled. Nothing like that ever happened again. I believe it was a very misdirected chiding by my mother, and she realized it quickly enough. I also wondered how she concluded that my brother and I had differently sized penises since we were practically twins in that department. She was unpredictable, my mother, and for that I am forever grateful, but always on guard.

The light suburban chatter continued on Charlie's deck. My brother's in-laws covered the news report about sports and the convenience of their latest gadgets. My penis situation was no better having been talked about separately with my siblings, but at least my middle-aged life carried on in the New Jersey yard as the crickets started to chirp their sex cries. By night's end, it was clear that my brother and sister had conferred about my situation as they sang, loud and to the tune of The Knack's *My Sharona*, just before my exit to the Suffern train station, "My my my my Pa-rone-eez!" The magic of Mahwah. The safety of siblings.

When I told my parents about it that summer, while Adam and I ambled with them along the sidewalks of fudge and ice cream stores during a rented weekend in the Berkshires, they were concerned, solemn and thankfully did not sing. Much safer. Since they had been living with their own collection of scars, physical deformities, and fake joints—a weary pancreas for mom, donated cadaver bone for dad's neck, all chapters in their history of health horrors—they showed complete love and compassion. While walking through Lenox, I asked my father about his father's Dupuytren's contracture and if he had anything wrong with his, you know, situation below. His first response was that he thought his father's finger had been all bent over from an accident with a machine in the carpet factory where he had worked in Yonkers. My mother said to my father, "You know your father was always making things up."

Later, at dinner in Stockbridge, the subject of erections came up. I wanted to give more graphic detail about the deformity. While Adam was in the bathroom my father told me he never let himself have one any longer because his foreskin had adhered to his head so the pain was too great. I knew he had developed adhesions—he is a good advertisement for baby circumcision—but I had no idea it had stopped him from having sex. I could imagine his penis trying to poke its turtle head out, getting all pink and peppy—and then, just as it was getting to that three-quarters feel-good moment, he would have to think about The Mets or lean up against an ice block so his foreskin would not rip apart.

I had seen my father's penis a couple of times in the locker room off the indoor pool of our Poconos clubhouse in the vacation development he optimistically bought into. My brother and I were ten and eleven years old. It turned out to be a good place to learn to ski and to hang out with kids from Valley Stream, Long Island. I loved all the salamanders and local ferns and made large terrariums in five-gallon glass water jugs. My brother loved to swim all year long in the indoor pool behind glass, sun or snow outside. We would swim for hours. We took saunas. For middle-class people it was luxurious. There were no private changing areas. My father was very shy, a former altar boy, and the first time we all had to change together near the lockers and cedar sauna, everything smelling like chlorine and Finland, I watched him look around for a place to change privately. This would have meant jumping into a bathroom stall. He assessed the situation and across his face blew anxiety followed by the confident acceptance that it would be better for his sons to perceive him as relaxed about nudity as opposed to ashamed.

He dropped his bathing suit in front of us, took a shower, dried off his thin, pale, hairy legs, pink torso and everything else, and put on his daddy clothes. We saw his uncut aardvark penis, all hairy, about five feet away, as we tucked away our baby gerbils into our Fruit-of-the-Loom cotton briefs. The only other uncut penis we had ever seen was on Philippe, the tall French kid from our day camp with the pointy eyes and long Alsatian nose. Philippe was made fun of mercilessly. He was proud of his penis and showed French disdain for the American hooligans who teased him. My brother and I remained neutral. We were not bullying types. Plus, Philippe was a little older and more developed so it all looked pretty good to me.

Like Philippe, my father had a French-type penis in that Pennsylvania clubhouse locker room and my brother and I did not make fun of it. We did not ask about it. After my father put on his clothes, he was a little aggravated by having to live outside his comfort zone. I felt newfangled with my cut penis compared to my father's old-world member. I felt that without a skin wig covering up my head, I would have a freer, more confident life. I had a modern, winning penis.

Adam still not back at table, my father finished telling me about his penis adhesions. "No booze, no smokes, no sex. Why don't I just kill myself?"

Though the words were strong, his temperament was light.

Adam returned from the bathroom and we changed the subject to safer fare like the décor of the grand old room and the goodness of the meal. But the pain of life's decay lingered. My mother has spent much of her life facing down obvious and mysterious diseases. With insight, she melts in warmth and empathy whenever one of her children has an illness and is happy to listen to our struggles and to offer advice. She is harsh and bottom-line about what she perceives as shortcomings in many of the people she is related to, but give her kid a broken toe and she hugs and gives like a medieval saint. But you can't stay home forever and you do have to face your illnesses while living in the greater world.

We ate dessert. Adam was very cheerful and loving toward my parents. They always enjoyed his company. Adam had an espresso. I drank a cup of tea. I could do nothing about my parents' old age. They could do nothing about my middle.

I was at a party in a good friend's substation loft in Los Angeles, the location that stood in for Mark Ruffalo's restaurant in the movie *The Kids Are Alright*, talking to two older straight men about memory loss. They were ogling the hot young blondes at the party who were not ogling them. I was trying to connect and relate to these two duffers. Gray thinning hair, consolidated energy. I was excitedly telling them about a book I had read and I could not remember the name of the author—and now I cannot remember the book—and I ended my part of the conversation by having to remark on the decline of the brain as one ages. The taller, dryer man, stirring the ice in his drink said, "Well, that's the second thing that goes."

·5·

WAR

Missing the Throne

I waltzed in for my first Verapamil treatment.

Somewhat resigned to misfortune but also excited to get on with it, I entered the waiting area. This was not ambivalence. This was mild depression propped up by optimism. A gay pair in their fifties sat on the yellow leather chairs with blond wood arms. They were cute and, like many couples that need a break from each other with a hit of something new, they both checked me out. It felt good to be wanted visually even if I was nothing but a distraction from their anxiety or dullness. This disease gave me fears of sexual implausibility on all levels. I have always used sex as something to slip into whenever I have felt generally bad about myself, my career more specifically: a built-in biological ego booster. From age sixteen onward I was the kind of guy who could have sex easily. I was good-looking enough, with my Western Euro-mutt face, strong jawline and tight body, to be worth grabbing, but not so good-looking that people were intimidated. Naturally, years made me fatter and my face has lost its sharp edges, but I have retained the spring in my step as someone who once was able to walk into any hotel lobby and catch someone's eye and then go upstairs to take care of business. It was the ultimate acknowledgement, getting undressed, watching some guy get heated up over me. This is not shallow as much as it is primal. And fun. Those exact days are long gone, but I always figured there would be someone, maybe older and plumper, who might still want me in a pinch. Even if I could never take off my pants in semi-public again, these two trawlers in the waiting room made me hope that, at least clothed, I might still enjoy future hits of recognition. The pursuer in any future sexual realm may not enjoy the jester hat-shaped thing between my legs, but dressed, this clown might still amuse.

I wondered if the relationship of these two sitting men was anything like mine. I assumed they did not have any children. They did not look fatherly. When you are in a relationship without children there is no chance to escape your disappointment with your partner by making school lunches. Daytime is often lonely for me. Daytime with Peyronie's disease was extra lonely. Adam was busy and happy at his new job but his stress level was increasing. This was not only because I was going through a diseased passageway or due to the rigors of his new gig, but also because his father was heading toward death.

Adam's father, Bill, was in advanced stages of Lewy body dementia, the second most common form of dementia after Alzheimer's disease. Lewy body proteins, named after the man who discovered them, Friedrich H. Lewy, cause a build-up of plaque in the brain, depleting the neurotransmitter dopamine. This causes Parkinson's-like tremors. For additional enjoyment, the brain chemical acetylcholine is depleted, causing a downfall of perception, thinking and behavior. Bill shuffled around his house, often did not know what he was doing, lost his way in the middle of a sentence and had not been able to play a game or follow through on anything with a beginning, middle, and end in over three years. However, he did not forget who he was, where he was or who anyone else was. This was partially cruel. Some people with advanced brain deterioration can become unaware and "happily demented." Not him. Bill wore a constant depressed scowl, not unlike the one Adam often sported after drinking two martinis while I castigated him for not paying attention to me.

Adam, with his three sturdy sisters and his healthy mother,

Carol, had meetings with a geriatric social worker down in Baltimore. Bill and Carol had always lived together. Since Adam's parents' marriage was never a winner, with a dryness between them that almost concealed their hot resentment, it was clear that Carol was not going to move into assisted living with Bill. The social worker and anyone else with eyes could see that it was time for Bill to have constant supervision. According to the social worker, it was not uncommon for a healthy partner to remain home, to not move with the failing partner to assisted living. Plus, Carol puttered in rooms and rooms of yarn, cut-up rags, journals, and spices and spent her hours crafting, scribbling, cooking and generally enjoying moving from one creative workstation to another. There was no way she could fit her stuff into a small apartment in some complex.

I was amazed at the callous way the family was ready to throw Bill onto an iceberg, sending him off to the old folks' home in the faraway state of Idaho, where Bill and Carol used to live. I thought the least Carol could do, if she was not going to live with Bill, was to take an apartment nearby and spend a few hours each day with him. It must be known that Bill was most likely a closeted homosexual, as revealed by his notebooks that were marked "trash" but were not trashed. The writing did not reveal enough to know if he had ever acted upon his impulses, but he fell strongly in love with at least one man while married to Carol.

Bill was also a sourpuss and a raging insomniac, but he did work his pointy-headed physicist ass off at DuPont, unhappily, forever, and had provided Carol with a great nest egg and pension upon which to live out her nut shells, piles of reading material, hooked rugs and celery strings existence in a comfort known to few. The least she could do with the cranky old cuss was move with him to Idaho and assuage his anxiety over impending death. My projection. My anger. My fear of being alone at death. What happened to matrimonial duty? Everyone was so ready to be rid of him. No one liked Bill that much. He was historically mean. But I liked Bill. He was old and mellow when

I met him. We talked about science while the girls and Adam shopped. I never saw the young angry man. Surely, Adam's mother must have suffered plenty.

My vitals were taken. I was called into the procedure room for my first Verapamil treatment. John, the nurse practitioner, came in and greeted me. He was bald, gay and calm and I was glad for that. John walked out, brought in another nurse, this one blond and female, and while she pulled my penis taut by the tip, John took a medium-gauge needle and stuck it into the shaved base—I had shaved back the edge-hair the night before per instructions—and for about twenty seconds pressed down the plunger, pushing the numbing Lidocaine into my mellow submarine. He then kneaded this hot burning liquid toward the distal end, the head. I was pre-warned of this heat sensation. It was, as they said it would be, the worst part.

I waited alone for fifteen minutes while my penis became completely numb. I like numbness. It reminds me of how great it is going to be when I am dead. No more bills. No more flossing. No more wanting. No more disappointment. With this kind of non-feeling, I could win this war. I have always liked living. Just a psychological break every now and then would have been nice.

John returned, alone and with a smaller-gauge needle, punctured my penis just below the head on the left side about thirty times, squirting the Verapamil and saline solution that would soften the scar tissue. John said, "The scar tissue feels good and granular."

I guess that was better than bad and slab-like?

Afterward, tranquil John put pressure on my penis with a gauze pad, sopping up any blood that came out of the needle holes. He said, "This minimizes bruising." He wanted to make sure I knew he was not holding onto my penis just for something fun to do.

Then John wrapped up my penis in a tight bandage.

"Leave it on for one hour. You can take it off at home. This will stem any bruising, too."

It looked like a beige mummy. Done. The procedure was bearable. I could take it. Just five more times. As a bad Texan president once said, "Bring 'em on!"

"John, I have to go to the bathroom. Can I go with this thing on?"

"You can urinate with the bandage on."

"Really?" I thought he must have been joking.

"Yes."

"Okay. Thanks a lot. That wasn't so bad. Thank you."

John nodded and left the room. I put on my clothes.

I really had to go to the can. The bandage was so tight, and as any five-year-old boy will tell you, if you squeeze your penis when you have to go real bad urine does not spring forth. In fact, thank goodness this option exists for kids in the backs of cars while a rest area takes forever to appear. I went into the bathroom because I was truly ready to burst. Note: Do not drink water for at least two hours before these treatments.

I stood over the toilet, my penis subcutaneously thick and heavy with the Verapamil/saline solution, swaddled into a light-purple response, ready to prove John wrong but anticipating relief if he were right. I had a heavy, non-erect five inches of liquid-filled manhood hanging over the bowl. Thick and pendulous, it felt great to have gravity working on me. I have been told by a kinky friend that some guys get off on injecting saline into their penises because it makes their members look large. Guys and their dicks! Women are right. It really is what we are all about. And if a woman had a dick she would actually know why and so many of the world's romantic misunderstandings would simply fade away.

My penis, the center of attention, was wrapped from stem to stern with just the urethral hole, the meatus, peeking through. I stood over the white, elongated hospital toilet. I let the urine rip forward. It hurt, like some sadistic Egyptian—or worse, Englishman—had reinstalled the Aswan Dam in my urethra. The dam did break under the half liter of urinary pressure but the hole was being squeezed and changed in shape by the bandage like someone chewing on a straw. The piss went everywhere in multiple thin streams. But it had to be done. I made a messy flood in the restroom as far as the curved edges of the gray speckled vinyl flooring that was coved upward against the walls. I cleaned it up with wads of paper towels and threw them in the metal garbage receptacle below the single-unit towel dispenser.

On my way back to Queens I called Adam. Our latest insurance, the third plan now because Adam's job turned permanent, was a mess and not going through. Adam told me that his insurance orientation at work had been postponed so that was why it was not yet working right. I yelled at him from fear. I easily feel unseen and unheard—another reason for the hotel lobbies and special wooded areas as a young adult, trawling for attention—and when I got home I texted Adam and apologized for my Edvard Munch scream.

Sorry I yelled at you, honey. It's tough to go through a time-sensitive medical thing in a sensitive area while changing insurance, twice…Going to sleep.

He texted back that it would all be taken care of within twenty-four hours. I thanked him as the Lidocaine wore off. I started to feel the dull throb of pain. It was not terrible. It was kind of like the pain you would feel if someone had stabbed your penis with a needle and then sharply poked away at some scar tissue just below the skin over thirty times. I have had much worse. Sinus infections, for instance, are far more debilitating. As is raw garlic in any meal since I do not have the enzymes to process it.

I lay in my bed in Queens and thought a lot about our house in Los Angeles. The quiet bedroom. The strange tree outside the window that gave radish-looking fruit in the spring for birds to eat and fluff in the fall for us to sweep. It gave me comfort. Our house was the most solid place we had and I was glad I could at least think about it even though at this point it was filled with tenants, two straight couples sharing it with, most likely, a grand total of two unbent penises.

Before and after I took off the bandage, I took pictures. My saline-engorged penis with all the liquid just below the surface of the skin was doing new and funny things. Edema. Purple. I squished the liquid around, thinking it would be better if the liquid were spread and shared so it would maybe absorb faster.

Dr. Hellman's original instructions were to ignore my penis for two weeks and not look for any significant changes. That night after the first treatment, after the liquid had been absorbed, luckily there was a positive change. My penis was straighter and looser. My mood immediately improved. I felt like one of the lucky ones. The bruising was horrendous. My penis was the color of an eggplant all around the upper portion and the skin looked like the saggy elbow of a ninety-year-old Sicilian woman. But I am not squeamish. Each day the bruising diminished, the pain diminished, the swelling went away and I was better for it.

·6·

THE SECOND AND THIRD REGIMENS

Castration Anxiety

Heading into the second treatment, I hoped I would see the cute older gay guys again for reassurance, though I understood this was statistically improbable. Instead, there was an even older New York woman cawing on her phone with that awful city accent that I do not find quaint, but is often amusing, "And he said how many years has it been since I saved your bladder? I said, nine. He's great, he's a great doctor. So nice." Then she went on with her grocery list. I let myself read the Jake Gyllenhaal article in an old *GQ*.

Once inside, anticipating the needles, the same thing happened to me that happens when I fly in airplane turbulence. I shut down into a nonreactive fog. This is a useful strategy to reduce anxiety, preferable to panic. This is not exactly a choice, but something my unconscious collapses into for my protection. Within minutes my visual awareness had increased because of the greater relaxation, though I had no emotional reaction to the surroundings. After the burning Lidocaine was shot into the base of my penis and the nurse exited, I could truly see the medical curtain with the upper one-fourth of fishnet webbing—beige with a hint of yellow in it, tan really—and then there was the solid lower section with mod, pell-mell-colored pastel squares with curved corners and soft edges. It all looked perfect to me. The designers clearly wanted to calm you down while giving you just a hint of something to do, to look at. An entire world of being-okay in a curtain. I was happy to lie there. Pudding in a cloud.

The procedure went snappily. I barely noticed it while in my plane turbulence-type torpor. I calmly told John, "The big bending is on the right side. The last time I had a lot of bruising on the left and a big lump of liquid underneath. I squished it around at home to help it reabsorb."

"Don't do that. The amount of fluid is below the penis volume limit. Leave it alone this time. You don't want to increase bruising."

So, I probably increased the bruising.

Then John went for it whole hog with his Verapamil needle—on the right. He stuck the needle in midway on top. Once underneath the skin, John poked the needle into the scar tissue twenty or thirty times. Swift and thorough on the right side this time, I wondered why he had only treated just below the head on the left side on the first visit. Was this guy a quack? Did he know what he was doing? Furthermore, what *was* the exact number value of the penis volume limit? What a crazy thing to say. He kept the needle in the same hole and switched the pricking direction north, south, east and not so much west. He was very quiet and then pulled out. He repeated this action two more times in two more punctured holes. John wrapped my stabbed penis super tight to stem bruising and the pooling of liquid. The bandage pulled on some hair—Shave closer next time, kiddo—I was floating.

As I walked to the subway to go home, I was happy that Lexington Avenue went downhill. Less effort. I streamed with the crowd on the sidewalk as one of those New Yorkers with a secret. I was walking with the working crowd but I had this completely mummified wiener in a neutral beige wrapper—which was shooting down my left leg in my Ralph Lauren Polo granny panties, one pair from the stack that I bought because I read that briefs were penis constricting and not a good choice for Peyronie's sufferers or any man—but I couldn't feel it because of the Lidocaine, just the engorged weight of it. I liked that it felt heavy, monstrous. I knew I had better stay away from schoolyards because my face doesn't lie. I called Adam at work and left a message. "Everything went okay."

I was forced to walk down three broken escalators to the F train. Multimillion dollar properties above, no money for mass transit below. On the subway, I had to stand. Some woman bumped into me with her clanging pocketbook. I crankily asked myself—Why all these huge purses?

I was very careful getting out of the subway. I lingered behind, waiting for everyone else to clear. I did not want to be bumped into so I put a serious space cushion around me. I thought of that classic 1950s driver's education film that shows a huge Chevrolet. The sexless nerd in club master glasses narrates that it is essential to leave one full car length of distance in front and behind your car for every ten miles an hour of speed. People are dangerous. I walked home the nine-tenths of a mile to my apartment. Queens is quiet and there are trees and squirrels, especially the farther north you walk away from the elevated subway tracks on Roosevelt Avenue. Inside, I took off my clothes. An hour had passed so I took off the bandage.

Blood! Coming out of three holes on the right. I took pictures, sopped it up with tissues and waited for the clotting to kick in. Why was I bleeding this time? I continued to question whether this whole gig was nothing more than a scam. John had done most of this second treatment by feel, pricking around under my penis skin like a teenager rummaging for a pack of cigarettes hidden in the lining of a winter coat. Had the ultrasound been inconclusive? Was this all a floorshow and would my penis get better over time anyway?

Then I questioned my questions. Could this distrust be arising from nothing more than my desire to find a motivation to stop these treatments? I did not want to have blood leaking out of the sides of my penis. Panicked, again, I shut down like I had while looking at the beige-and-colored-squares curtain and I fell into a cloudy distance. I do not trust people, it appeared to me. Especially with my penis. I wished I could be more relaxed about it, but I could not.

The blood clotted. The saline was evenly distributed this time. I did not squish anything around. I did not bruise as much. Okay. Good. Thank you, John. I was still floating near the ceiling and I talked myself into staying on course with these treatments. These probably were not witch doctors. I just hated to have to continue with the truth that my primary pleasure center had been put in the hands of businesspeople. This was *my* penis, after all, and I had always loved it, and it felt past treacherous to hand it over.

In the tenth grade, I was lying flat on some wrestling mats. Our public school educated a large district and the tax revenue was ample enough for the building to be outfitted with a planetarium, an Olympic-sized indoor pool, an enormous theater, music rehearsal rooms, shops, gyms and a wrestling room with every inch of the floor covered with mats. It was also the weight room. The gym teacher—Hey Coach—had us sit on the floor in the beginning of class so he could talk to us about joining a sports team, telling each of us to pick one as an after-school activity. Some of us were lying on our stomachs, chins in our hands, looking upward. After a minute or two, rubbing against the mat, I had a complete erection and continued, subtly, to press it into the mat against my hairless belly. I could tell the gym teacher was going to talk for a long time so I would have a while to bring it back down. I thought—This feels so amazing and I feel so alive and I am so very happy that I do not even care that I am in gym class. Nothing else is bothering me when I feel like this. What a great built-in thing to have. Forever. And I am not going to join a sports team. I'm going to act on the musical stage.

The coach, all hairy-armed and wild-eyed, asked us by a show of hands which sports teams we were going to join. Cross-country, soccer, football, all that. He also alluded to the winter sports, the baseball of spring. Boys were all excited. They were born for being physical in these various ways. Finally, he asked, "Who didn't raise their hand for any sport?"

Three of us raised our hands: me, my erection down by now, and two other guys. One was very thin with a sunken chest, a real sternum problem. The other one weighed a jillion pounds. The coach asked each of us, "Why not? What sport do you think you could do?"

The malformed kid mumbled something about cross-country. The very large kid agreed that that would be good for him, too. The coach looked at them with a warning smile that he had better see their names on the signup sheets. Then last but maybe not least, "And you?"

"Well, I'm not going to sign up for any teams."

I was embarrassed, being put on the spot, but I was also determined to enjoy high school as an academic, a thespian and a singer and to not be bothered with this stupid kicking, sweating, ball chasing and panting.

"Why not?"

The coach was incredulous and was using me as an example, the Don't Picture.

"Because I'm going to be in the school plays."

Snickers. Smiles.

The coach pressed on, "Really?"

"Yes. I would rather do that."

"You could be on a team, too."

"I don't want to. I want to save my time for school and for the play."

The misshaped boy and the big boy had glee in their eyes. They were glad I had spoken up. They signed up but never joined the cross-country team. Even though I was a complete loser in the athletic department, I felt proud that day. I had stood up for myself and imagined that maybe other boys, not just the athletic outcasts, were impressed that I had been honest about my true nature. Plus, my brain was still happily bathed in leftover boner chemicals. This trumped all other pain or shame. That was all the physicality I would ever need.

I was surprised the coach did not applaud me for being different from the other boys while still maintaining a shred of positive self-regard. In elementary school our gym teacher, Mr. Broom, all Dry Look, white-blond hair parted to the side, never tried to embarrass me for being a complete hand-to-eye-to-ball klutz. In fact, one day he had had it with all the shenanigans the kids were pulling—getting out of control, not listening to him, throwing and kicking ropes and balls around like wild animals. He blew his whistle and made us all sit along the perimeter of the gym. One wall was foldable. In fact, you could unfold all the gym walls right into the cafeteria, where there was a stage. Mr. Broom admonished the class, incredulous at how rowdily they were behaving. In a quick blow he said, "Now Donny Cummings,"—he was the first person to ever call me Donny, so sweet, something Adam took over years later— "Okay, he's not so great at sports. But he listens. And he is respectful! Take notice!"

Mr. Broom was furious. I was the Do Picture in elementary school. In gym. I thought this high school coach in the wrestling room would have let me be who I was, too. Maybe even have applauded me for my particular personality. But I am very simpleminded in my associations. No chance. The high school coaches were much more serious about physical prowess. Well, I had my boner and my music and my Krebs cycle. So please, the rest of you boys go get dirty in the fields.

Two Verapamil treatments were completed.

I continued to wear my stretcher, the AndroPenis, as prescribed, four hours every day. I wore it each morning right after Adam went to work. If I did not get four hours logged in in the morning, I would complete the remainder at night when Adam and I were watching television, the head pulled by the strap, my penis nearly stretched into the next apartment. Adam kept a warm distance. He appeared neither optimistic nor pessimistic. He was being respectful of my problem, thinking it best that I take care of this slog without too much input from him. I would have loved for him to hold my hand. Sometimes he did rub my feet. But only when the stretching session was over. Too much moving around and the polymer lasso that held the penis head ridge could slip off. This often happened when I made breakfast or sat at my desk to answer emails. The penis, or at least my penis, tended to get a bit slippery when plastic rubbed against it. The penis skin can get quite a yanking during the stretching, which Dr. Hellman warned could make it a little bit ugly. Mine was not too bad—I'm a bit oily in general, which is good—but I did notice some longitudinal stretch lines. I creamed up the shaft with cocoa butter before bed.

Adding the half-centimeter screws every week, I was already up to ten centimeters on the stretcher. The AndroPenis was especially helpful in keeping my penis straightened in between treatments. More importantly, I felt like I was keeping my length. Peyronie's disease has been described as strong rubber bands under the skin, pulling the penis tighter and shorter. I was hell-bent on fighting this action no matter how much time it took. Plus, having your penis stretched is sexually uplifting no matter the kind of manipulation. Pre-cum often came to the tip after ten or twenty minutes of stretching, something to certainly clean up. The sadness that came from the visual of having my penis in a medieval-looking torture device was counterbalanced by the mild physical arousal. It felt good to parade around the house in drawstring pants, my penis sometimes stretched straight up toward my navel (easier) and sometimes pushed straight down toward my knees (more difficult). I always started upward and worked my way downward. Ninety degrees from the body was not an option. Too boinky. I was afraid I would bump into edges of tables or chairs in that geometry. Two treatments completed and many hours logged in stretching, I was going to win.

Then I had the dream.

For over twenty years, I have had this recurring dream that I take off my penis as if it were made out of clay, or really something more like Silly Putty, and then put it to the side to be reattached in a few minutes. There's never any blood, only pink clay skin. I take it off as a game or to clean it, like someone putting dentures into a glass of Polident, or, usually, because I am trying out something playful and new. It's my toy after all and I do like to experiment. Then I try to put my penis back on, to make it stay put, but there is always the question of whether or not it will heal into place. I know I have to take it easy and to give it time, maybe a week. I make sure the severed urethra is lined up and the clay is sticking. I anxiously wait—Will I lose my penis for good?

Sometimes I panic and I'm terrified that I've messed up for life and should have never played with my penis in a removable game so I decide to rush off to the emergency room. I have such remorse and almost as much fear as I have in another recurring dream where I kill a homeless guy and bury him in the woods with my brother and Nola, my friend since junior high school, and the cops start sniffing around. A toe has surfaced out of the mud. Jail for life right around the corner! Oh, these stupid mistakes I make in my dreams!

It is always so awful to have this dream where I have pulled off my own penis. I always wake up before I even get out of the house to get to the emergency room. It is just me with my penis barely stuck on, the clay barely adhering. There is the hope that the penis will remain attached and heal. It is never resolved.

In this most recent recurring Silly Putty penis dream, my penis came off just below the place where they had stuck all the needles that day. I basically ended up with a headless shaft. I could not get the head to reattach. This accident happened because I stupidly dry humped the back of someone who looked a bit like Mark Ruffalo—whom I once met doing a reading of *Summer and Smoke*—and a bit like a friend of mine's boyfriend, in an attempt to cheer him up because he had not been having sex for a long while. After that simulation, I went into the bathroom and I took off my penis head at the Verapamil needling spot. There was something new about this recurring castration dream. My penis had a small tongue and groove notch for reattaching. Possibly an improvement over my past versions of this dream?

Well, thanks for the notch, but I still had trouble. I kept

trying to reattach it, but it kept slipping, turning, not adhering, even with the small tongue in the groove. So I came into the living area—which was now a 1970s deck house, all low-slung, burnt-orange wood and Bauhaus-y—where my mother was getting ready for work and my father, brother and sister were in sitting states, not doing much, but also about to start their work and school days. There they existed in their normal lives while my urethra started to spout semen like an Arkansas hot spring—like it had been in there all built up waiting to jet for months. The semen made my penis very slippery, which made it impossible to keep the top piece in place. I knew I had to go to the doctor immediately, but the question was—Do I go to the emergency room or to Dr. Hellman? I was worried about perceptions and loyalties. Would Dr. Hellman feel slighted if I did not go to see him? Or would the emergency room people think I was nuts to be doing all these Verapamil treatments to my penis? Time was wasting on my penis clock as the semen made it impossible to reattach the head, and I wanted to be liked. My need to please at the most basic level could have destroyed me. Everyone knows that in an unattached penis dream, if you do not get your penis to heal into place the day it is severed, the cut-off piece will rot and die.

Then, like every other time I had had this dream, I woke up, never making it to the emergency room, the question of the penis healing unresolved.

The whole night I had been having very painful erections, the pain mostly on the left side. The head of my penis was pushing up against the band of my underwear, putting pressure on the shaft, making it hurt even more. But in the morning, lo and behold—I looked down and my penis was straight and also still a little chubby from the liquid injections. The right side where there had been the spilling blood was now a double orzo-sized lump. The skin over the lump was very white, but my penis was attached and it even felt good. I hated that dream, but I loved that my penis was looking a little better.

The next night, I took matters into my own sexual hands to

see if things were working. My penis was fully straight and a lot of the pain on the left side had subsided. I masturbated to the medium-priced porn that Adam had chosen for us online and it was not a horror show. Jerking off upward, gushing, it felt good.

The third treatment, two weeks later, was old hat. It was September, a great month for renewal. I had a 10:30 appointment so I was unusually awake by 8:00. This was Hurricane Earl Day. The beast was hovering off the coast of Virginia. It was breezy and very humid. I had to wait ninety minutes to get into the office.

When I was finally put into a room, the nurse practitioner, Ms. Slope, came in. Again, she took great care to be conscientiously sensitive. This was the first time she was going to give me the actual treatment. The day before, while looking at my printed schedule with her name on it and anticipating this appointment, I had had a fear that her secret desire was to mutilate my penis. I thought of my close lesbian friend Nola, the person I sometimes murder homeless people with in my dreams. Nola came into lesbianism later in life and had had much sex with men. Now, she holds penises in such disdain, finds them so disgusting, elephant trunk-like and wormy-vile that when she talks about them she sounds like she wishes they would all just disappear and like she would be happy to make this happen, with her scythe or chain saw—It's my penis, Nola, just let it be, no? We're friends!

Ms. Slope settled me in. Dr. Scavone, who did my original ultrasound, came in to inspect. Grim. Not a smile. Then Dr. Hellman actually arrived to give my member a look-see before treatment. He asked me how I was doing. I told him that for the past two weeks my penis had been perfectly straight.

"Maybe we should not do the treatment since your penis is fine."

As he was talking I realized by his tone that he was saying this only because he thought I was there for my first round of injections. While inspecting my subcutaneous plaque, I got the sense he was having a memory problem so I snuck in sideways, "You know, the third time you do anything, you really get used to it.

It's my rule of three."

Dr. Hellman smirked, confessed he did not realize this was my third time, and said that we should go ahead and do the treatment.

"We don't know whether it's the Verapamil treatments or the AndroPenis stretcher that's giving you the positive result. If it had been the stretcher only and you hadn't yet had any injections, we would not begin treatments. But since this is the third one, we'll continue."

I thought how if I were a doctor, I would never make a mistake like that. I would always look at my notes. I'm vigilant. Dr. Hellman only came in to look at me because he happened to be there. He was not scheduled to see me, but still, we were talking about my penis and I wished he had not come in so forgetful. Was there no protocol? No charts or anything? Everyone flying around by the seat of their pants?

Dr. Hellman had to throw out wrappers on the counter. He told me, to soften the distance between his mistake and my horrified face, "I have OCD tendencies. I get it from my mother."

I wondered if he was gay. Admitting he had a problem made him seem more human to me, so possibly, in my biased mind, I thought he could be gay. Straight men do not often admit to any vulnerability. Some do. Very old men, Jewish men, the insane, but not most. I like confessions and I felt more comfortable. He tugged a lot on my penis. He said the tunica and the scar tissue were starting to have the same consistency, so it was getting better. They numbed me and left for fifteen minutes.

Ms. Slope returned and administered the Verapamil-saline needle. The easy part, really, because of the numbness. She said, "We don't know much about this." Her tone was that of the gentle helper of Dr. Frankenstein. We talked about our relationships. She told me about her wife living up in Northampton, Massachusetts and about her own apartment, about living in Brooklyn and how her wife was raising the three kids she showed up with and how, she, as a nurse, had to live in New York for the money but her wife, too, could make six figures here instead of the thirty K up in Western Mass., but the kids ... She was very kind during the treatment and she did not appear to want to hack off my penis. There really are so many kinds of lesbians. I made a note to remember that. Also, to be more aware of my surface associations and my bigotry. The new generations are so much better at this than I am.

After finishing, she told me to take off the bandage in an hour. Now that was a consistency that made me feel calmer.

I was optimistic on the sidewalk heading back to the subway and very hungry—Oh look! A sausage cart! I ordered a sausage, but while the vendor was napkin-ing it up I realized I did not have any cash on hand so I said, "Stop, please, I don't have any cash. Sorry."

She just got mad and scowled.

"I'm sorry." She did not care how sorry I was. I walked away. New Yorkers, with their time and money over everything else. Okay, so I caused her to grease up a bun. The sausage would still be usable. She would live. But now we sort of hated each other?

In the subway car back to Queens, I had the recurring thought —I've got a bandaged up, freshly needle-pricked secret, so scandalous. No one come near me please. It's weird and it is by far the most sensitive thing on me right now. You don't want to know about it!

As I walked home in that largest borough, space bubble around me, the weather got weirder from Earl, so thick and moist, and I wondered if there would ever be any relief! As a storm blows in, if you are in the center of it, you may get very focused and alive. I was happy and my mind slowed down. Come on, Earl.

At home, I took off the bandage and this time there was no bruising, no blood at all, no pain, and it looked like she had injected much less liquid than anyone had before. More finesse, this one? Or maybe the office was just collecting money and really doing nothing more than injecting saline and not Verapamil since I was already so much better? Who knew what was happening? This treatment could have been a placebo? No matter what, my penis had become straight and the pain would eventually go away and it was plumping back up so this was all very positive. I was halfway through my treatment schedule. I still was unsure if this office, this best-in-the-Peyronie's-biz-bunch, was nothing more than a bunch of cock quacks. But things were getting better so I figured I may as well accept happiness in finishing out this ride so I could get back to some sort of sexual glory. So I could still give Adam the good sex he deserved for keeping me in cabbage, care and fun. Pleasure, anticipated, is often more thrilling than the pleasure itself, like Macbeth before the murder—*Oh, Happy Penis, handle toward my hand, Come, let me clutch thee!*

But, you just cannot know, in this dark kingdom of the penis, how it will all turn out.

·7·

POETRY OF THE PENIS TRIUMPHANT

Rod McKuen

The fourth treatment was on the first day of autumn. Beautiful, but I was suffering from terrible GERD. The acid was up in my chest, throat and sinuses. I could imagine the clear hydrochloric acid burning up my neck and head membranes. Whenever I lose weight this happens, the opposite of the proclamations of health articles. My allergies were flaring, too. Time of year. All systems down. I arrived at 3:02 for my 3:00 appointment. A guy in the waiting room, short, Hispanic and darkly appealing, was kind of eyeing me in that horny-bored waiting room way. He had thick brown hair. It felt good to be checked out, again. The sexy lift eclipsed the medical dread of the day. And if we were to sneak off together, I'd even be able to show him my nice, straight, reconstituted penis and he would show me his and we would celebrate them together, no matter what his trouble was. I was so happy I was not the last person on earth. I was able to share energy with another guy, be it sexual or otherwise. We were both willing to engage. This happened in the good old days with greater frequency.

The subway broke down. A common occurrence in the 1990s

in New York. Used to such a thing, I was prepared with a book. Across from me sat a man with an open boyish face, something I've always liked, with straight silky chestnut hair, something I liked even more. He wore a business suit and looked good in it, like my father. This made me feel safe. He watched me through the dim emergency lights. We were at the far end of the gray hard plastic seats, between the double door entry for the platforms and the single door that exits to the next car. It almost felt private. His pale skin, dark eyes, oddly small nose and flat Mongolian face with high cheekbones confused me. I could not place his ethnicity. I thought he was one of those hot Hispanics, like the actors you were starting to see in the movies who were becoming international stars. Antonio Banderas and Andy Garcia. He was a little bit overweight. I was rail thin. I knew I had a chance. He was cute as hell.

Even his shoes turned me on.

There were announcements about the train, how something was being fixed. Some override. Or some redundancy. Or someone maybe even pulled the emergency cord. Did it matter, really, what happened? The trains were always breaking down and there I was across from someone with an incredibly charming smile and very pleasing hair. The MTA was giving me a present. In blinking amber light. A few times it went black. No one was scared. We all just took it. The suited stranger's eyes were lit. He was getting a little hot in my direction.

Once I knew I had his attention I put on my show. I was subtle, I think. I did not complain about the stalled train. I wanted this suit to know that I could handle distress with ease. Which I could. Which I did. I smiled, crookedly. He smiled back. I made small commentary.

"This could be it. For the rest of our lives. I hope you brought a sandwich."

He continued to hold his smile. He was vulnerable and bashful about flirting in opaque public. This, of course, made it even better. The train sat there. I used to sing a subway song to myself that summed it up—*The RR is for Rarely Runs. The N train, that one Never comes. The E is Eternally late, The F for Fuck it, why even wait?*—I would save that song for a future subway ride with him to Coney Island.

We were stuck for forty minutes. I continued with my young shenanigans and he continued to be shy and cute. His bright eyes never went dim. We both wanted entrance. He gave me his card. Louis. I wrote my number on a piece of paper. I liked being the scrappy one, improvising with whatever was at hand. The burst of feeling you get from the possibility of a new person, a new life, a new something, ran up and down my spine, into my head and into the hand that wrote my phone number. God, I loved his smile. I had been so alone and ready for interaction. Even my father, on the phone the previous Saturday, had said to me, in response to my glum mood as an invisible single, "A person has to spend their life with someone else. I don't care who it is. Go out and meet people."

Sex combined with love and intimacy was always my higher goal. I was excited about the man of the subway blackout and ready to get back on a horse. I had suffered through a three-year relationship in my early twenties that required three years to get over. We were simply too young to be together, Eric and I. We were both actors from the middle class, ambitious and domestic. I was from the East. He was from the West. I loved his huge penis. (But why is everyone a bottom?) Because we were so young, our penises were hard as rocks and no one ever gave a thought to future penis troubles. We had sex a few times a week. We kissed a lot, rubbed our dicks together, sucked each other for fifteen or twenty minutes. Then he would get in position to be fucked and of course, being an obliging sort, I would fuck him. I can still see the smooth, hairless skin on his back and shoulders that I would look at while I pumped his ass from behind.

Afterward, I liked to watch him squat in the tub in the kitchen, spraying himself down with the handheld nozzle. Even after the sex was over, I would still be aroused for him. I could look at the monster between his legs all day long. We men, with our visual cortex hooked up to our libido—it's very enlivening.

And endless. Bottomless? Endless. He was a sweet young man with romantic ideas of one day owning a nice house with a few big golden retrievers galumphing around. Until then, it was a tenement walkup for us. We were in very young love.

But there was some trouble, the least of it being career competition.

We both auditioned for *Equus*, that horse-fucking play that never made any sense to me. Callbacks required nudity, which under equity rules was illegal. This was not an equity production. We were both up for the lead role. Eric's dick was larger and thicker than mine, but more importantly, his flopped around while mine did not have that kind of stable-like heft. Eric looked British. He got the part. My jealousy was hot. It turned out that Eric was miserably unhappy in the play. He did not like all the attention. I was certain everyone wanted to have sex with him and I was probably correct, but Eric was a very loyal boyfriend and also loathed objectification. It made him very uncomfortable, like someone was taking something away from him. My parents saw the play. I was proud this well-hung, young Richard Chamberlain type was my boyfriend, but the distance between us started to gape. When he was at rehearsal, I was thinking about how to separate our stuff. His unhappiness was unending. I was rowing upstream, trying to make him happy. "What do you want to do? Which TV show? You want to go out? You want to stay home? You want to go for a walk? You want anything at all? Should I jump off the roof?"

Like most gay men of the period, we each struggled with self-loathing. Eric was paranoid and felt everyone was out to get him. If the grocery store did not have ground beef for his recipe, he went ballistic, as if the whole world was conspiring against him. For my part, I wanted great sex and complete fusion. I was overbearing, but perhaps I could have been less so if I had actually received some affection besides the few sexual acts each week? No change of my behavior would change Eric's behavior. His father tyrannized him growing up so I was perceived as the current tyrant taking up the cause. Eric was miserable living with me. He hated being an actor. He had to make a huge change. I could not stand how unloved I felt so I broke up with him twice. The second one took. He moved back in with his parents. I remained in our small walk-up apartment on 99th Street with the bathtub in the kitchen and cried for months. I wrote a song about it, which I performed, which everyone told me sounded like a variation of a Joni Mitchell tune, which made me feel unoriginal.

Time, right? Time. After a lot of acting work out of town and figuring out how to celebrate being single and enjoying the company of other actors who were also single, I figured out I could be by myself and even enjoy not needing others to love me so much. There was the clapping audience. I knew it was not real love, but it was energy. There were the jokes in the green room, horsing around with theater comrades, and the soft late-night admissions of vulnerability on tour busses. I did Moliere, Shakespeare, played the Tin Man in *The Wizard of Oz,* learning that I had had a heart all along, no matter my relationship status. But after each performance, after the curtain had come down and everyone had gone home, there you were, the public persona cliché: alone, just you. So even though I could have continued to run around the country in small theater productions, getting surface recognition from audiences and enjoying the group play with the other actors, what I really wanted was to stay at home and experience real love with one real person. My father was right. I needed to meet another heaving being. Eric was long gone. I was glad the lights had gone out on the MTA and something new was brewing.

Louis, the adult subway foundling, called me the next day. Oh, to be called! I really wanted this, and I would actually be doing something based on my father's advice for the first time in my life. That felt good. Maybe this would be the guy for me. How fun would it be to tell future friends and family that we met on a broken-down subway?

Our first date was Indian food. I love a man who loves to eat in a restaurant. Until the Louis period, during my late twenties, in my walkup and on the road, it was mostly frozen fish sticks, hot dogs, ramen noodles and flavor packets. I sometimes got wild with relish. And here he was, a stranger I had met on a subway, with a job, in a suit, who was happy to take me out to eat. Louis and I rollicked in bed for hours at a time. This was much better than the short bursts with Eric. Louis wanted to fuse with me. Louis was incredibly affectionate. Louis touched me *all the time*. I was open-minded, in a mood to give back and ready to be completely codependent during sex. By his nuzzling and fervor, I could tell Louis had to have something more than the usual. I intuited what he clearly needed. "What do you want? What do you want? Let me give it to you. You want me to hold you, little guy? Make you feel safe?"

With that, he said, "Yes," and then he burst into tears. Even though I was young and in love-need, I had a feeling this sobbing might become a problem. His damage, something that expressed itself in tears post-coitus, was surprising, intriguing and the tip of some wretched iceberg. But I did like to try on hats. Or better, even, lend a warm gloved hand. Maybe this would be good for me, to not be afraid. I would just have to pay close attention. Wasn't it sweet that someone could be so vulnerable during sex? I felt vulnerable most of the time. But after sex, I usually felt strong and calm. I needed to know a lot more about this Louis.

Louis was not Hispanic. In fact, he was an old guard WASP from the Midwest with his dark hair gelled into a shine, nothing more. He worked for an insurance company on Fifth Avenue, near Bryant Park. He had had a few relationships that did not work out. I had had my failed relationship with Eric and a few other shorter excursions. His parents had a time-share so he swapped a property and took me to Gurney's Inn out in Montauk. We had the largest little house right on the beach, romantic as all holy starfish. But before we got on the Long Island Railroad to its natural termination, Louis had to tell me about what was going down in his therapy sessions—Sure, Louis, tell me. We're all New Yorkers here—Plus, something was going on so I did need to know.

Louis was a sex addict. This was not shocking as so many gay men become "addicted to sex," or what I like to call, "Without human women around we can fuck like bonobos." But there was something real about this defined addiction. Eventually, he got used to having sex with me and the boyish tears dried up. He was comfortable and safe. But as soon as we would finish up he would want to start up all over again and again and again. There was no way to continue. After you've been going at it for three hours, what the hell is left? A glass of wine and an omelet, I say. I was limp like a shelled bivalve mollusk, but Louis just kept coming at me with his oyster knife.

His situation was more severe than most homosexual cases of "sex addiction" because he had had a more sexually severe childhood. At twelve, his father taught him the birds and the bees by jerking off to climax in front of him. As an introduction to the process he said, "I'm just going to show you." Then, after he had come all over the place, he said, "And that's sex."

On Saturdays, when Louis's mother went to the beauty parlor for her hair appointment, Louis crawled into bed with his otherwise verbally abusive father and they had sex. Every Saturday. For years. His father arranged the entire thing. Louis admitted this made him feel special. To have a screaming father who bullied all of his kids single you out for such special attention, well, this was like a prize. It was sexy. It was secret. It was consistent.

When Louis was in his mid-teens, his father brought home truckers he had befriended at a local stop and had them pile on top of Louis like the hot teenage boy that he was. There was a network of traveling pedophiles and I guess swapping out your son was something they did in those days. Upon learning all this, I was aghast and amazed. Could I really handle dating someone who had been continuously raped like this? I would like to say that I felt terrible for him, but like some victims, his sexuality was informed and energized by this constant rape. It charged him up. You could see it in his eyes when he talked about it. It was complicated.

"I don't know if I can handle this," I told him.

"Oh, James—"

He called me James. My middle name. I liked the way he said it, sexy and warm.

"Louis, really. I mean, even when you talk about this thing with your father, the truckers, you seem excited."

"It was exciting. That's the problem with this kind of thing."

"So, you liked it?"

"Yes. But I'm not alone in that."

"I understand."

"James—"

He kissed me, looking into my eyes. I was James, the kid he was now comforting. I was the first boyfriend he ever told about this childhood mess. I was the one who could handle him during this healing time.

"Oh, Louis—"

"James—"

Now he was saying James like I was someone else. He had left his body. The discomfort and draw of the past pulled him into a trauma state, I imagine, and I was a distant person of his creation that was safe but not necessarily real. Nicknames are controlling. He was placating me with a tone that said, You are a nervous little guy, you can do this, don't be so scared of me like everyone else.

Ambivalent. I could never supply the energy it would take to compete with the negative force of his father's destruction. I wanted to be optimistic. I mean, people have gotten over worse? Louis could maybe pull this off. I was very attracted to him, this damaged man-boy. I wanted him to take care of me in an old-fashioned way, in his suit, with a steady paycheck. In return, I would hold this damaged little kid, his somewhat flabby but still very attractive body, in an effort to soothe him. I could give him the care his family had denied him. Maybe. Tentative. Scary. Shit.

I flew to California to see if Los Angeles would be a better city for me than New York. I visited my cousins Bernard and Bernard's wife Caitlin in San Diego. Louis's father and mother were living there, retired, so we met. Louis set it up. He somehow wanted me to see that his father was not a monster. This may have been some sort of Stockholm syndrome on his part, where you relate to your captor, but much more involved. I met them with Cousin Caitlin in tow, telling her the entire backstory before we arrived. She, like me, was all roused up in an investigative reporter kind of way, as we trough-pigged at a suburban all-you-can-eat salad and buffet chain restaurant. The conversation was American mild. Louis's parents were old, gray, paunchy and saggy and looked like they should have been sitting on big lawn chairs at a medium-sized lake. The father eventually got to the subject that made his eyes come to life.

"I like to hike out in the Anza-Borrego desert, east of San Diego."

Years later, when I drove to California to live, I drove right through it. It was on fire.

"Is it a national park?" I asked Louis's father.

"State. I think. You in town all week?"

"Yeah."

"If you want to come with me, we should go."

I nodded one of those, *Oh yes, we shoulds* ... and shortly after that, the check came. Caitlin and I got out of there.

In the car Caitlin smiled pleasantly, trying to lessen the blow of this surreal encounter. "I can't believe he asked you to go hiking with him."

"I'm not surprised."

"Oh, Donald."

My family has always called me Donald.

"It's fucking insane, right?"

Two nights later, I had a birthday dinner with my cousins at The Marine Room, a country club restaurant in La Jolla on the ocean. Louis had planned it so his credit card would be charged. It was lovely. He really was generous. But he was working me. I was in Southern California but my encounters were too Louis based. I was feeling trapped. I returned to New York, secretly knowing I could easily live in Los Angeles and could not wait for the day to get out there.

Months passed. The sex with Louis calmed down as he was getting off with other guys all over town. Two times, he came home late from a business meeting in a leather jacket, with a cat-who-ate-the-canary grin that signaled, clearly, that he had had sex with someone. He didn't try to hide it, wanting me to accept him for who he was. I was furious. He apologized and cried but still was elated for having had the sex. I told him this was probably not going to work out, us. Louis begged me to stay, standing there in the cookie-cutter kitchen—in a tower in the East Nineties, in the early '90s—of the apartment he was subletting from a friend of mine. I was not necessarily against extra-relationship sex. I was more concerned that he had so little control over it. It made me feel like I could vanish at any moment. Or, let's face it, like he might give me the disease of the day that was killing everyone.

Louis begged me to meet with his therapist so that she could explain to me how getting over a sex addiction was a messy, slow process. I met with her on the second floor of a red bricker in the West Forties, on Theatre Row. I listened. As she made her case for Louis and his progress, I made my case for every fate that could befall him, and then me, given this psychological, action-oriented minefield.

"He could go out every night and have sex with someone else. I could be invisible forever, the only thing in his head his father, or the truckers, the thrill of anonymous sex, blocking out anything we could have together. He could get herpes. He could get AIDS. He could kill me with it. He could lie to me about all of it. He doesn't lie, exactly, but I know he doesn't tell me the whole truth."

She either played naïve or was naïve and said, "You have quite an imagination."

"Maybe I do—," I said, cooperatively, trying to give her the response that she wanted. Therapy is like a big improv game. You pretty much have to say "Yes" or the scene stops. I do have a big imagination and I can reach for the hysterical, but death is real and it was all around us and I did not want to die. I was offering up worst-case scenarios, true, but hell, not only was the grim reaper stalking us from a medium distance, there was my own up-close relational psychology to deal with. When you have abandonment issues—and who doesn't if you grew up in the selfish '70s, raised by parents who were very young and very busy getting out of their own personal internalized ghettos of shame, like I did—you have to take care of yourself. I survived my own lonely childhood, the booming AIDS epidemic and more by being super self-protective. I said to Louis's therapist, "I just don't think I have the time for this. I don't think I can do this. I don't know. I'll try. I don't know."

I soldiered on another two weeks.

Louis's job, the insurance concern, sent him to Washington, DC for a business trip. He kept a journal. After his return, he left this journal in the middle of my friend's sublet bed. It screamed to be read. He wrote about having taken a huge penis in his ass in DC and how good it felt to be completely overtaken and manhandled like that and how Don was not adventurous because Don did not like Ethiopian food. I decided to confront him to finally break up with him. Louis came home.

"We have to talk."

Louis was smiling. I was certain he had just had sex with someone else. He was wearing the tell-tale leather coat.

"I read your journal."

"Why?"

"It was on the bed."

"You shouldn't read my journal."

"Yeah, I know. But you left it right in the middle of the bed, like you wanted me to read it."

He didn't say anything.

"So, you had a good time in Washington?"

"Sometimes. Sometimes it just feels good to be taken over."

"I know I don't have a huge dick."

Louis did not answer. I could not give him what he wanted. I had always felt a bit cheated in the cock department. I had the confidence of someone with eight inches while I actually just squeezed by with six, the average, or what I learned recently, from the most conclusive study, is slightly above average (but they did not include Africa). Louis had a look on his face. I had one on mine. It was over.

I continued, "Ethiopian food is not for me. I have a bad stomach. I don't like to sit on the floor when I eat. I hate that spongy bread. And I hate eating with my hands. It's disgusting. Who cares? So what?"

Louis reached toward me, took my shoulder. "Oh, James."

"Shut up with the James. I feel like an idiot. This is over."

"No."

"Yeah."

"James, no."

"Louis, yeah. I'm done. Go fuck whoever you want. I can't take it."

Louis started to cry. Not that hard.

"You'll live, Louis. Your therapist is fantastic. You can do this. But I can't do this. So I have to go."

I slept over that night, with Louis, in my friend's bed. We had sex one last time. It was sort of sweet. I only got half hard. In the morning he was even sweeter.

"Are you sure?"

"Yeah."

This messy ride with Louis in the early '90s got me to think about my own possible sexual addiction. Like when someone dies and you take on their personality for a bit to keep them alive, after our breakup I imagined I was as sexually addicted as Louis, or at least in the same camp. I tried that on for a few years, which brought me almost to a halt in the orgy of life with anyone who wanted to get into bed, or bush, with me.

Eric, my first real love, once figured out that I had had a small fling during summer stock in the last year of our relationship. Truth is, the entire last year of our cold relationship I was looking for sex all over the place. I wrote that off as the natural response to living in a love desert and being twenty-six years old.

But maybe I was a sex addict, too, like Louis, and just hadn't accepted it yet? After our breakup, I went to two meetings of Sexual Compulsives Anonymous. I did not relate to the guys there. They were wasting entire days trawling for sex. This was not my trajectory. I just went out when I had the need.

The more solid fact I learned, and not to be glib, was that I could not date men who had spent a lot of time having sex with their fathers. It was a terrible situation, Louis's childhood. Perhaps I was selfish to hang in there at all, to think that he could become my well-behaved office worker, strong and reliable, so I could be taken care of a little. Was it right for me to want someone to be someone that was right for me? I also like to stick around until a story naturally ends. It naturally ended. Years later, we are Facebook friends. We respond with Likes or LOLs in each other's comment sections. At least he uses LOL. I find it disgusting. When I see his face, the cute dark-haired incest survivor, I do wonder if he is still in turmoil. I think he must be. Most people are.

The Hispanic guy in the waiting room looked over and checked me out again. Sweet. I gave him a half smile. My name was called. Vitals checked. Penis numbed. I waited fifteen minutes. John was very nice and easygoing. He poked forty or more Verapamil-saline shots into the scar tissue. He was holding my penis with medium pressure for a long time afterward. He reminded me he did this to stem the bruising. My warmth sensors were working. I felt my penis to be warm. I felt one of his fingers on my scrotal sack which was slightly sexual, but mostly calming and comforting. I asked him what was going on.

"You're bleeding a lot. I was aggressive with this treatment, but you should not still be bleeding. Are you taking vitamin E?"

"Yes."

He said, "Stop taking it. It's a blood thinner."

—Hm. Dr. Hellman said the vitamin E would not hurt me. This medicine world is more an art than a science, sure, but with the hard facts it seems like no one gets the memo.

I told John how straight and lovely my penis had been lately.

He said, "If that's the case—about forty percent of men react positively, like you did—then we'll continue to do six more treatments after the last two."

"Really?"

"And another erection inspection in between."

I sunk back—Good Lord! Surprise! I had thought I only had two more to go and that would be that. But I was much more relaxed about it. It was working. I could take the ache. I would rather have temporary physical pain than long-term emotional pain. John gave me gauze to sop up any blood if there was any leaking after I took off the bandage at home. I found a dollar on Lexington Avenue as I headed to the 63rd Street stop.

On the subway, I did not think about my wrapped-up secret. I felt safe being on the F train back to Queens. Then an overweight girl with a little mole on her lip, her hair back in a ponytail, white-skinned, tightly clad in rack cotton, was very aggressive about getting deep into the train. There were so many people standing in the car, I did not understand why she thought her efforts would yield anything. When she got in behind me she was audibly disappointed there was no seat for her. Full angry person with all reason evaporated? With my vulnerable penis, I had to get away from her and her big bag as she flailed. Her public display of emotion made me angry. In shared, tight spaces I make myself as flat and invisible as possible. Why couldn't everyone be like me? I edged over to the end of the car, away from the door. It is always safest there, the fewest number of people. I always think of Louis whenever I am at that end of a subway car. LOL.

At home, I had to pee so badly. I loosened the bandage a little before the allotted hour was up so there would be less pressure, so I could. When I took the bandage off, a little blood dripped out from the same spot John had been pressuring, but nothing alarming. It was good to be taken care of. By someone. Oh, John—I do love nurses. To be cared for, in some way, and to care in return, this was always my desire.

After my break up with Louis, I dated Billy. The night after my last night with Louis, I went out to the only bearable Upper West Side gay bar. This one was called The Works. It had a plumbing theme. Sort of sexy, sort of industrial, sort of urological. Billy was there hanging out. I knew him and it was comforting to see a friendly face in a world of strangers. Plus, I knew he had a crushy thing for me. Billy was sweet, a tap dancer from a trailer park in Michigan. We were introduced by a mutual friend who had worked with him in the entertainment wing of a cruise ship, the same friend who sublet her apartment to Louis. Billy occasionally wore makeup and was very thoughtful, but overly sentimental and, let's just say it, controlling in a whole new way.

Rebound Billy hated any sexual disloyalty and made it clear he would not put up with any of it and demanded full disclosure if I were to so much as graze a man's thigh by mistake. During the ten months we were together, he would freak out if I was late for dinner. I was always late for dinner. Eventually, I gave him exactly what he didn't want but insisted on hearing: all the details about how I jerked off with a stranger in a car at a rest stop on the New Jersey Turnpike coming back from visiting my Aunt Ellen. Billy's eyes tightened in dread. He went ashen.

After ten months, we finally broke up when I was late for another one of his overly loving meals. He could not comprehend my thoughtlessness. I did my best to be on time. I was even on rollerblades. But he would have none of it. He felt too unsafe and his anger grew elephantine. As the fight progressed and I just had to escape, he said, "If you roll out of here, don't ever come back."

I rolled.

The next morning, he came over to my apartment. The fight continued. We moved it outside. I was in my skates again. He could not let anything go. He could not believe I was late for things. He could not believe I had a life outside his meatloaf schedule. He grabbed me, being entirely annoyed that I was rolling faster than he was walking. I fell, cut up a few fingers on the sidewalk, played up the drama of the abuse and told him, as the tears streamed down his cheeks—he was not wearing mascara at the time—that we were officially done. Our sex had been pleasant and mutually giving, our penises evenly matched, our bodies in good shape. Gratefully, there was no sobbing coming from him after we finished having sex. He was well-adjusted that way. His father had only been verbally abusive, not sexually. But Billy was terrified of being abandoned and made it impossible for me to do anything but leave. There was no love there. I left.

Then I fucked two other guys—we all agreed that's all it was—who did not know about each other for four months. One was a Mexican flight attendant with completely smooth skin, thick black hair, a beautiful, large, international manhood and a need to be topped. (Everyone really is a bottom.) He also had a silly sense of humor and wore too much cologne, and all his friends were, sadly, uninteresting, at least to me, but he loved to climb up onto a chair, put his ass in the air and have me enter it. I loved every minute. To make someone so hung that happy made me feel I was substantial. He was always clean.

The other one, a cute white guy living with his parents who wanted to build his own business as a nightclub promoter, I saw less frequently. He had a German name, was entirely American and sported a large *Mitteleuropa* penis. Another bottom with a young tail to tell. He had already graduated from college and was biting off the question of how to get his own place. I could not help his living situation, not that he was asking. I did want to rescue this chomping lad, but the most I could give him was temporary horseplay. I was close to leaving town for Los Angeles, for what I thought would be forever, and had a futon bed set up in a loft in a freelance photographer's studio in Chelsea where I was working as a studio manager to eke out my last few weeks in Manhattan. I gave him the good insert, with my young, perfectly straight, thick, cut, six-inch penis, right on the futon, right on the floor, as an early version of a Mac computer blinked its screensaver overhead.

Then I moved to California, where I would soon meet Adam.

Penis at the ready, my twenties were behind me.

Home now, in my forties, in Queens, after my fourth Verapamil treatment, Adam emailed me.

How is your rod?

I responded.

Well, today was such a poetic experience, I like to think of it as my Rod McKuen. Honey, I think it's all about timing and mine has been great. Basically, I went in at the perfect time, so they will just keep attacking me with stuff as long as my body is attacking me with stuff. It's going well, really. Two more to go!

The fifth treatment was in early October. A rainy day. Nothing special. I had been noticing that as my penis was increasing in length from the four hours of wearing the AndroPenis stretcher, the new skin section behind the head was getting very white. At the doctor's office, it was Ms. Slope again who greeted me. The appointment was at 1:00 and I was not seen until 3:00. I fell asleep in the waiting room.

Dr. Hellman performed the treatment. I got the sense that Nurse Slope had been demoted but was still needed for nursing support. She seemed too eager to please Dr. Hellman and had a supplicating style with him that made it appear to me like she had recently done something very incorrect. Dr. Hellman said to me, "You are an early responder."

"Great."

"This means that you should be tested again for curvature after the next time and then we will do another six treatments."

So John wasn't kidding.

Dr. Hellman said, "There is no data for people who did well and stopped after six. It's a gestalt thing."

I think what he meant was it's a gut feeling thing. Or gestalt can be used in this way? I wanted to get to the bottom of the cause. I was calm, but I still wanted reassurance. I asked him, "Why does it only ever happen once in someone's lifetime?"

"They think it's an autoimmune response and may be a response to injury—I did research for years for a viral thing, thinking that the virus lives in the tunica and when there is an injury it's activated. But there was nothing conclusive."

His story was consistent.

"Do people with allergies get this more than others?"

He said, "There is nothing like that, but it is a population thing. Like cats with their version of FeLV."

He reiterated the Northern European white guy tendency. He asked me what I was writing lately. I told him about a play and then he said, "I had an interview once from a writer who described me as slight and intense. My mother read it and said, 'What's he talking about? You're not slight.'"

I like men with problematic mothers. They are often more interesting than the ones who have had it easier.

The treatments were bearable. They just wore me out. I went home after the fifth treatment. My penis did not look bad when I unwrapped it. I ate Adam's leftover meatloaf and sat there, tired. I thought of my father who always said, "Don't let your meat loaf."

Mid-October, I had my sixth Verapamil treatment and all went well. My appointment was for 1:00, then was switched to 4:30, and then they called back to say come in at 1:00 to see the doctor, and then another call to wait until 5:00. I rolled with it. I spent the day on the phone with mortgage brokers for this insanely operatic dump of an apartment we were not going to buy on West 47th Street. When I arrived at 5:00 it was dead quiet which was good because nothing was in the way and it went fast. Dr. Hellman came in.

"This is going to be your last treatment."

"Oh?" He had been saying for weeks that I should come back in to do six more since I was a success story.

"Your penis is straight. You should stop now and come back in three months for a curvature assessment."

It was so frustrating and scary that the treatment schedule was so mutable. I thought—Why does he change his tune all the time? Then I thought—Who cares?! What a relief to be done with these treatments! I could now live freely. I asked Dr.

Hellman, "If I were to write something about this, could I come talk to you?"

"I get hammered in reviews of my work. The community wants control groups. I won't do controls with placebos, obviously."

"Of course."

"You'd be doing people a big favor if you let them know about this. You know, Bill Clinton has the disease. Jennifer Flowers talked about it."

Who knew if this was true? Maybe Monica? I understood William Jefferson Clinton wanting to use his penis more often if there was a chance that his sex life could diminish to nothing. If Bill did have this disease and if it had gone untreated, as I mentioned earlier, the plaque could have calcified, and then you have big trouble, perhaps even the need for an operation. The classic surgery is called the Nesbit procedure. It can also be performed at early stages of the disease, but it is not immediately recommended by most doctors.

The Nesbit procedure involves girdling the skin of the penis just below the glans and pushing it down out of the way to expose the tissue underneath. Next, you pinch tissue on the opposite side of the scar tissue, cut some out and sew it up. Then the skin is pulled back up and sutured in its original location. This slightly shortens the penis on that opposite side so that the snipped side is equally compromised in length. With this surgery, after your penis is healed, you have erections that are straight, though perhaps a centimeter or two shorter than they were back in your halcyon days.

I did not hear about Bill Clinton's bent penis in either his or Hillary's memoirs. No one gets an advance to contract Peyronie's disease and then write about it. Few have gone gonzo about their own penises. How strange, this Peyronie's disease—so common, yet we rarely hear about it in our oddly sexless/oversexed culture. Wishfully perceived to be rare when it actually afflicts one to five percent of adult men, it is not even in spell check.

After my sixth treatment, I went home and took off the last bandage. Lots of blood and saline came out of one puncture hole. Then it stopped quickly. Staying off vitamin E, the blood thinner, was the correct advice. When they are poking holes in your penis, clotting is essential. And then, it looked like I was done.

I was able to have sex with Adam normally. I could give him what he wanted. I was cautious when we had sex. But I could make him happy with my straight penis, delivered straight up, into wherever he needed filling. Adam looked so young, relaxed and happy when he was taking it and I was so glad that I could make that happen for him. He worked hard. He deserved sexual pleasure. We all do. We were fortunate to be living in New York City, surrounded by great medical care. Adam would not have to hire prostitutes or seek out strangers for a solid fucking. He could settle for an almost as solid fucking from me, like in the old days. Since we had been together for so long, he knew what to do to max out my hardness. When to work the nipples. When to work the shaft. It was so great to be in a long-term relationship. Perhaps we could grow old with our sexual relationship intact. And more.

·8·

THE LIBERATION OF FRANCE

I Rue Dupuytren the Day

These treatments had mucked up my schedule so there was a backlog of demand for travel. Most of October and November were spent out of town. Los Angeles for business and old friends. Baltimore for Thanksgiving with Adam's family, their favorite holiday. In between, walking around Paris, it felt thick and strong to have blood filling my penis with weight as it swung loose in my gigantic underwear. I remembered well this penis, while vacationing in France. Like the involuntary reminiscence of a Sunday *madeleine*. This trip to Paris was a chance to show my cousin Bernard's kids around a city I loved and knew well. Four men, two middle-aged, two in their early twenties, seventy-five percent with normal penises, twenty-five percent with a penis that was almost there. Coincidentally, our hotel was in Place de L'Odéon which is intersected by Rue Dupuytren, named after the doctor who first introduced the method to operate on scar tissue in bent fingers. I wore my AndroPenis stretcher less frequently when traveling and then much less in general. I was glad to be done with my ridiculous twist of fate. We enjoyed the Paris tourist sites, walked all the way to Marie Antoinette's Trianon from the Hall of Mirrors at Versailles, ate loose ham-and-cheese omelets for breakfast, and went home.

By late November, while in Baltimore for the holiday, my penis began to shorten. This was a surprise. It became a little tighter toward the front half. During an erection it would tilt to the left. Dr. Hellman had said this often happened, that the penis would go one direction, then the other, then tilt upward. Before long, it stopped tilting toward the left and it did tilt upward. But then a great distortion afflicted my penis and I became extremely upset, with a kind of deep discontent that never gave up for one minute of any day.

The new shape took over very quickly. During erections, though the base was quite normal, the distal end, toward the head, became tightly constricted and started to narrow exponentially. It felt like I had two penis sections, one on top of the other. The bottom half was thick and fine. The upper half flopped above a new constricting scar tissue ring that grabbed the center of my shaft like a mean horseshoe. The top three inches just below the head shrank to what looked like a newborn mouse. That part was extra pink and hung on like a desperate beast over the top of the normal, thick old-fashioned area of the bottom of my penis. The upper baby mouse continued to get smaller every day. This latest, horrifying, scampering attack of scar tissue on my tunica albuginea, turning my penis half human, half miniature rodent, chewed away at my self-confidence so that I stared at walls and hoped one would simply grab me, pull me inside and suffocate me. My penis, in addition to being scrunched inward at the top, like a milk bottle, had now become fully one inch shorter during erection, down to five. Shortly after taking this measurement I started to drink heavily.

Red wine, apparently, does not help matters, but I needed to escape. It was one of the random Peyronie's websites that said to stay away from alcohol, mushrooms and a few other foods. What the hell did any of these people know? They were grabbing at straws like everyone else. I uncorked the bottles of red and got down to business. I drank every night and became depressed and hopeless. To have quick success followed by swift, greater deformity and to then attempt escape through ramped up addictive behavior was a recipe for suicidal ideation. I knew I would never pull any trigger, but I did feel myself leaving my life. My playwriting career was stalled and frustrating, as so many playwrights over forty who are not famous have experienced. Whatever. I had a penis to take care of. According to a certain Peyronie's disease guidebook—which I purchased online and which I was instructed to stay away from by Dr. Hellman, who said it was hogwash—it was important for me to use hot compresses on my penis every day. I did that every morning. It did help to loosen the tissue and to reduce pain, but it did not make the matter go away. My milk bottle would not be delivered from its shape.

Like looking at cloud formations while lying on a lawn and seeing Scandinavia or a cow's head, I asked Adam what he thought my penis looked like during erection. I suggested a milk bottle. He said it looked more like a shortened torpedo. Who needs oily splotches on a road to discover and define surprising images when you have a penis that supplies all the pareidolia you could ever need? I did not call Dr. Hellman. He had made it clear that I should not do anything but wear my AndroPenis and see how things turned out after a few months. Aiming to please, by following doctor's orders, I got through the holidays. They were grim. I continued to drink. I did not do much else.

I knew my sex life was over, or at best, some sort of freakish event that could only ever end in self-pity and shame. Since I put so much value on sex and feared disconnection, I imagined abandonment was inevitable. Unlike the hot stump of an amputee, no one would ever want this thing even for kinky sex, so it would just be me, living this experience, ashamed, disgusting, alone and unwanted. I was a failing hunchback. I was a lady with the arthritic fingers and the chin wart with the hair, going unnoticed in aisle six. I was a guy covered with boils, condemned to live in an unheated room above a garage in a decaying industrial city. I was H.G. Wells's *Invisible Man*, unseen, with no social or scientific upside. I was a disembodied hook arm rusting in a ditch, a baby with the exposed brain, a walking teratoma, which is that awful tumor loaded with eyes, hair and teeth. But really, worse.

I was a man with a destroyed penis that no longer became erect in the upper half, which was smaller than it used to be and was terrifying to behold. Adam would have to have sex with me out of some sort of duty, not desire. Our sex life ceased.

I tried to find what could be positive in this situation. It certainly made my partner's penis look amazing to me. I used to have the good car; now he had it. It also slowed me down to a forever halt in the out-of-town sexual tryouts with others. Plus, hadn't I always been a bit oversexed, over-obsessed with my body, overboard in general? Maybe this was my wakeup call. But I did not wake up. I grew more sullen, withdrawn and alienated from people. I would walk in Central Park and look at young men and think about how Thomas Mann surely felt in Venice. I experienced myself as a phantom with no friends. I thought it would be no big deal, really, if I were to leave the bio-bag that was my body. Since that is where we were all headed, anyway, I thought—Why not just get there sooner than later?

It felt like death, the end of my sex life, or at least a sex life that would include my penis.

Luckily, I had faced down some severe mental states in my life. It was time to pull from my reserve of experience. I hated being depressed and anxious. I had to elevate this mood. Being in my forties, I had lived long enough to have plenty of archival footage stored in my psyche from the earlier days of distress when I needed to save myself from wretched psychological ills. I could search the vault for a picture of relief.

During college I almost went crazy with facing the truth about my sexual orientation combined with the pressure from my mother to become an engineer or a physician. The gayness was uncontrollable. With regard to one of the sciences as a career, my mother was being practical and was doing the best she could. I was not. I smoked mountains of pot and, during my sophomore year, joined in with a group of outlying guys in various stages of unhappiness who were enjoying the harder hallucinogens.

My first trip on mushrooms was filled with love. We young

men spent the weekend in a beautiful brick colonial in Newton, Massachusetts, appreciating nature, or at least the bushes, feeling warm toward each other, sure that if everyone on earth took mushrooms there would be no war. That Monday, hoping to escape the chemistry and biology labs of Tufts University as soon as possible, I hoofed it to New York City and auditioned to become an actor in the program at Juilliard. I performed a monologue as Biff from *Death of a Salesman*. I was not accepted.

The second trip, on mescaline, was on campus, and everything grew alien and pointy. Tufts is a bit Victorian in places so it all got a little spooky. Plus, I had body trips, feeling like if I stretched I could reach for miles. I could sense my internal organs. This was not enjoyable.

The third trip, slurping from a huge mug of mushroom tea, landed me in the hospital. I had the dreaded death trip. I was convinced that I had consumed too much of the drug and I hallucinated that I had died. Severe anxiety took over. I spoke in tongues. I was inconsolable. An ambulance whisked me off campus to Medford General.

At the hospital, I was convinced that the white-gowned men were devils hell-bent on holding me down for eternity, that hell was a place where you had no control or power over yourself. The worst part was the idea that it would never change. Eternal damnation, I guess. In real time, they were only holding me down because I was thrashing. A huge shot of Valium brought me back to reality. I immediately sank into humiliation. My parents drove overnight through an ice storm to be with me. My father sobbed. My mother realized I was a gay, career-terrified mess. I had severe panic attacks for years after that which always made me feel like I was going crazy. I had to make myself not crazy. I had to choose *not-crazy* every day.

It was mostly my own will that made this possible. When I would begin to fade away into an anxious spume while walking around campus after dinner, I would use a very angry energy to yell at myself to come back to the living. I gave myself small slaps on the cheek, usually on the right side, to shift the energy.

It worked, or just riding it out worked. There was no control group called *Don-bis* so I could not know. But this is what I had. Naturally, I had weekly appointments at the counseling center where all the other overachievers, anxious wrecks and depressed anorexics were battling it out with their inner demons. And many more years of therapy after that. Eventually, I did become happier, joyful even, and powerful. I had to. I was too young to let go of life.

So maybe by sheer will I could lose having a sexually functioning penis but somehow remain content? Self-insist that I change my morose mood? I did not feel like visiting a New York City psychotherapist. So sick of shrinks. Maybe I could rearrange my world view so that being sexless, with a piece of dark-orange dried apricot between my legs, would be nothing to be sad about or ashamed of, but something to manage and then accept. A tall order. They say when people lose things, they eventually get back to their baseline happiness level once they get used to the loss. The things they say ...

So now that I had thought about it, longing for youthful men in the park, remembering that I had gotten through a very emotionally tough scrape in college and survived into later joy, I emailed Adam. I liked giving him processed versions of my inner life since unprocessed feelings could overwhelm him. Introverts get drained easily. I heard, from Facebook, that being an introvert is like living in a human-sized hamster ball. They don't really come out of it. You eventually have to make them feel safe enough—making sure not to be overwhelming—that they let you into their ball. Plus, this message gave me the chance to try to become more positive, though I was wobbly.

Honey,

I swear—my dick is getting tinier and tinier—I fear that our sex life could end this year. I have decided that since I could end up with a very strange erectile situation—to the point of micro-penis, or worse, a twisted micro-penis—that I could either get super depressed about it or look at it as a chance for spiritual growth. Or something. That would be good. But I have to be honest, it's difficult. With this particular area of my body going into a necrotic state I do feel much closer to death. And because of that, well, I guess I feel like death coming sooner than later would be good. I'm sorry, but that's how I feel. I wish I had better news. I think, though, that I am glad I started to have sex so young—because at least I have memories of lots of good sex, with a normal penis that was not in a state of shriveling up into a piece of tiny driftwood. Strange, to have this happen. Thanks for being there. No need to keep saying "It's okay, don't worry about it." That oddly makes me feel more alone, like you're ignoring it. Basically, this whole inflammatory body of mine has turned against me in the most cruel way. I feel like the sooner I let this body go, the better off I will be. I am so glad I did not have children.

Don

Like the paralyzed character in the movie *Breaking the Waves*, what made the most sense was for me to let my man go have sex wherever he needed to sail. We were not the kind of couple who harbored jealousy.

We never flaunted anything at home, but in the middle years of our relationship, from our mid-thirties to early forties, if either of us were to end up in a steam room or on a massage table with someone else and that experience led to orgasm, no one really cared. Of course, it was a full Don't-Ask-Don't-Tell setup. And who is anyone to deny anyone else a well-hung Brazilian or anything else, for that matter?

Additionally, I came out at twenty-one and Adam did not come out until he was twenty-nine. I had begun enjoying myself so young that I had already had sex with, okay, hundreds of men and three point six women. I always thought allowing Adam some responsible free reign would make him feel less trapped in our relationship. Since I was his first real boyfriend and he had not had the chance to fully sow his wild oats, it just made sense. Because I had always been someone who liked sexual attention and sex and felt that such inexpensive pleasure was something I was not willing to release, I was lucky to be with someone who was as easygoing as I was about the whole thing. Of course, it was not just about the sex. Emotional incongruity was also at play.

About two years before my penis went into rebellion, when we were still living in Los Angeles, we decided to close up the relationship. We came up with the idea together, figuring it would make us feel closer to each other. It did make the sex at home better. But it has always been a murky area. In general, I recommend an open relationship for younger gay men after being together for a couple of years. Men, especially gay men, are penis-obsessed and like to offer it up. I was aware of this at twelve years old with the neighborhood boys, and with anyone else who took an interest.

In high school, when I was more interested in music and theater than anything else, like most men of my generation who were so inclined—to sing a song instead of throwing a ball—I struggled. This was the era before even one pop star or public figure had dared to come out. I did not know who James Baldwin was. People loved but still made fun of Elton John. There was no way to be proudly gay without risking a daily beating by jock thugs. I tried to be straight. It wasn't too difficult since I did have crushes on girls. But not for long. I knew something was up with men and I knew I was in trouble. Kathy, another choir member and the best actress from the class ahead of me, a member of my close social circle, fell in love with me. We were in plays together. My mother used to tell her friends, "They were dancing partners all through high school." We were a dancing couple once, in the Spanish Panic sequence in *Once Upon a Mattress*, when I was in the ninth grade and she was in the tenth. We were pretty good at it.

Kathy chased me for the next two years. I did not want her. She continued to chase. No one else was coming after me, which was disappointing. We went together on a class trip to Paris with our French class. She followed me around when I slowed down long enough for her to catch up. I ignored her because I was not interested. Many of my close girl friends were also on this trip. Kathy was less popular and more sensitive than these highly energetic, fun friends I enjoyed during my high school years. Kathy was not as irreverent. She was old-fashioned. Her goal in life was to have a husband, a house and kids. Maybe a job as a teacher. She was pale and dramatic, wearing strong stripes of makeup. There was nothing wrong with her—I just didn't want her. She was pretty and kind. She was soft and compassionate. She was well-read and talented. She was a loner and unpopular. I wanted rough and ready, rebellious and self-centered. I just wanted myself. Or some wild woman who wanted to destroy civilization. Or possibly, a guy.

Kathy's senior prom lurked. It was the end of my junior year. Many of my best friends were a year ahead of me. They were all going away to college and I was feeling the upcoming hole of abandonment. Kathy asked me to be her date. I said yes. It was an insincere move since I knew I was only doing it because she was my entry into the prom with all our best friends. I was surprised she did not notice my lack of enthusiasm for her. I would rather have gone with the sassy, neurotic, brilliantly tremulous Jane, but she was going with my best friend, Steve, a wonderful singer, who, too, had not yet admitted he was gay.

Once I said yes to going to the prom as her date, Kathy treated me like I was her boyfriend and expected me to behave like one. Hold hands in public. Come to her first with anything at all. Pay attention to her when she showed her living spark. I did it. I was in the adolescent souk and this was my only bargain. We sat together at our prom table at the Rockleigh Country Club, just across the state line in New Jersey: Steve, Jane, Kathy and me. The two gay guys and these two girls from the choir who were in the plays with us—we were not bound for love or glory.

The day after the prom, most couples went to the Jersey Shore. We went to Six Flags Great Adventure. I mostly paid attention to Jane because we were more apocalyptically suited to each other. Kathy was jealous. Steve and I would sneak off to the parking lot to smoke cigarettes and return to get on line for this or that log flume. Jane and I were loud and drew attention to ourselves, doing improvisational dance steps on the edges of the fountain on the fake Main Street. We were energized in that negative way where you get ramped up when you want to escape from your current hell. We both did not want to be with our dates and we both wanted to explode out of our lives. We did not stay anywhere overnight.

There was a long summer ahead. Instead of looking forward to her future far away from me at a college in Pittsburgh, Kathy grew more willful and doubled down on the push for me to be her boyfriend. That was that. I liked her but I did not understand intimacy at all. Plus, I was gay (bi?) and nervous. She was solid and dependable and taught me how to be consistent. I liked this consistency, as my choir and theater world, the most accepting place I had ever experienced, was breaking apart.

By the end of June, Kathy and I were boyfriend and girlfriend, and we became best friends. This was amazing, to have someone who I could depend on. It was one of those situations where I learned to love her. I never fell in love with her, but we did become a little family of two. What we had in common was a huge appreciation for music and acting and a fear of moving on. We both had unconscious knowledge, a foreboding that our personal futures were going to be difficult since we were both oddnicks. She lasted one semester in western Pennsylvania.

I felt guilty that I held onto her, on and off, throughout my senior year of high school and then during three intermittent years of college. I would say, “I have a girlfriend at the University of Connecticut,” which is where Kathy eventually landed. This made it possible for me to not be overly bothered with women on the Tufts campus. I was also geographically distant enough from Kathy that I could try out all sorts of sexual things without inconveniencing her. I could hitchhike to Storrs, Connecticut, hang out with her in her dormitory, smoke and have sex, then head back to Boston to my life of being bi-curious, but really boy curious.

Looking back, I behaved like a cad. At the time, I was terrified of living without Kathy's emotional support. Old-timey, she stood by me like a wife of yore. This was incredibly comforting as I was an emotional wreck about my upcoming adulthood. But worse, I did not treat her well. Christmas break my freshman year, she came up to Medford and sat in my room while I hung out with all the energetic, interesting girls on my floor, drinking, smoking and carrying on.

"Why are you with them? Why aren't you in your room with me?" she asked.

"Because we're leaving tomorrow for winter break and I'm going to miss them!"

This was true. I hold onto people and take too large a pleasure in never letting go. My need for those particular relationships on campus fully trumped Kathy's need for me to be holding her lovingly on my extra-long twin bed. She suffered through my youthful exuberance, putting up with my social mania. My best college friend, pre-med Ned—one of the guys to eventually join me in my hallucinatory mushroom trips, the guy who called the ambulance for me when I lost my mind—was surprised I was dating such a pre-Gloria-Steinem, zero-wave feminist. He did not know that underneath my fun, polymath, irreverent exterior, I really needed a solid, sober anchor. I was gay like the goose and was holding onto Kathy with both hands like she was some raft to my future heterosexuality on the shores of Normal-Land.

I was able to have sex with Kathy because I was young. Because I sometimes imagined I was with a guy. Because sometimes it just felt good. I worked at a truck stop as a short order cook in Mahwah, New Jersey and got her a job there as a waitress the summer after her prom. It was at the height of Springsteen. I wore white T-shirts and smoked Marlboro Reds. She smoked the same, in her brown polyester waitress dress, taking orders in the Lenape dining room. A totem pole always stood guard. It was for sale in the gift shop.

We had a party for Kathy on her last shift of the summer before she went off to that first college in Pittsburgh. Champagne and cheese were served on the stainless steel counter near the coffee makers and the milkshake machine. We got drunk. When we returned to her house we had sex on her braided rug downstairs in the family room while her parents slept upstairs. Being eighteen, alcohol did not have the power to diminish my erection. I was full, thick and throbbing, the head as strong as the base, one uniform tube of life force. Watching this power of flesh go in and out was as visually pleasing as the sensation. Unusually, I was doing her from behind, but in her proper hole, when she uttered, "I'm going to puke. I'm going to puke."

I was so close to orgasm, "Hold on!"

As she projected cheesy champagne vomit onto the floor near the television-as-furniture, I pumped a few more times, pulled out, shot on her back, and then heard her father, a conservative Republican supreme court judge of the State of New York, descending the stairs. He had come down on previous nights to check on us, so we always knew this was a possibility and we kept our clothes nearby in case. I quickly pulled on my clothes and ushered Kathy into the bathroom with hers, hoping she could pull it together as her father scooped ice cream, eyeing me from the open kitchen. She didn't pull it together. He found her on the floor of the bathroom, naked, next to a pile of her retched-upon clothing. He sent me home. The power of the pleasure of my penis, overriding all human decency, was supreme. I felt more embarrassed than ashamed. But I did not agree that vomiting should trump orgasm.

Kathy and I dated and had sex during my freshman year of college. I broke up with her early in my sophomore year because I did not want to be her boyfriend any longer. I had one of the worst years of my life with drugs and panic, those damn mushrooms, and was unprepared to be gay, so we got back together for my junior year. I spent the second semester of junior year in Paris, living in a sad lemon-yellow modern high-rise with balconies on Boulevard Soult, the ring road on the edge of the twelfth arrondissement, near Bois de Vincennes. Her letters would come. I was grateful that someone on earth truly cared about me, but I felt no connection to her other than what I needed for myself. It was ludicrous that I let her remain in my life. We had a plan that she would visit me at the end of the semester, but neither of us had any money so that never happened. I was often depressed in Paris, truly facing down my homosexuality.

I did everything I could to keep myself from having sex with men. I succeeded most of the semester, except one Saturday night when I hit the gay bars near the Centre Georges Pompidou and got it on with three different *mecs*. People want to fuck you when you're twenty. It all started when a roustabout in black leather leaned me over the bathroom sink, pulled down his pants, pulled down mine, left his coat on and pumped my ass with only spit for lube. It hurt too much. And Parisian bathrooms are small. I lasted a minute. Later on, another guy went at me. Then the bartender. I had to get out of there.

When I returned to my little town of Suffern, New York, Kathy and I spent most evenings of the summer together. I vowed to myself I would stay away from these creatures with penises, even though I was very drawn to them. Kathy worked at the truck stop that summer. I worked in the cafeteria at a state hospital where my grandfather was dying from dementia. I delivered his food.

"Tommy? Tommy?"

"No grandpa, I'm your grandson, Donald."

"Uh."

They kept him tied to a chair. He was a wanderer. Tommy was one of my father's brothers.

"Get this off of me. Get this off of me."

"I can't grandpa. It's okay. Eat your lunch."

I left him tied there and rolled out with the cart.

Years later, he died in that chair, the ancient Irishman with the Dupuytren's contracture of his right ring finger. Future Kathy, distant to me, came to that funeral. Her father had worked with my Uncle Tommy, the one my grandfather called for. Future Kathy was still as warm and kind.

I finally broke up with Kathy for eternity the fall of my senior year of college, a few years before my grandfather died. I was becoming more secure with my sexual orientation, which was brought about by trying to calmly have sex with men in and around Boston. Additionally, I did not love Kathy correctly. I was certain that I could no longer lead on this good person just so I could lean on her. I have been apologizing about Kathy ever since.

Like the endings of many tumultuous events, it did not go out with a bang but with a whimper. Kathy was concerned because I was so excited when I talked about my modern dance classes at Tufts. I did love them. Especially when I got to choreograph. Oh, to make things!

By chance, Kathy's grandmother owned a very ugly gray fourplex, built in the 1910s, across the street from our brick-and-shakes saltbox two-family built in the 1970s. My neighborhood, the working-class one in the good school district, had no romance at all, a kind of Kentucky-on-the-Ramapo, down-at-heel, blue-collar grid of ugly homes that looked like decaying farm houses, but pushed close together. The summer before my senior year of college, before the breakup, Kathy and I were standing in front of her grandmother's decaying building, the one that made my mother extra depressed as she swept the streets. I was on fire about my dance piece set to Brian Eno music, describing the moves in detail.

"And everyone loved it!"

Then she asked me, "Are you bisexual?"

What a surprise that was. I did not think she would be so direct, ever. I certainly was having sex with her. Who cared if I put on my dance outfit and had the time of my life?

"I think that might be possible, yeah," I said to Kathy.

"Well you're going to have to figure that out."

"Right now?"

"No. But soon. You're going to have to figure it out soon."

We puffed on our cigarettes. The neighborhood did not get any better looking.

"We might not make it," I warned.

"I gave you the best years of my life."

"We're only twenty-one."

She had not yet turned twenty-two. She wanted a professional husband, a doctor, you know? Who was straight. I made it clear that I was an artist and that even though I was going to apply to medical school, I really did not want to go. Her eyes were clear. I was probably not her man.

Back at college, I wrote her a letter to tell her I had not figured it out yet, this bisexual thing, but I knew we were over. She sent back a letter wishing me well. It was gracious. There was a tinge of fury. Our fizzling two years on, one year off, one year on relationship died by U.S. mail.

I did enjoy her company much of the time, mostly for the comfort and familiarity. I did enjoy fucking her. She liked to be fucked and I like it when someone likes it. Sometimes, I can even watch workaday straight porn and enjoy it. Something about insertion of any kind gets me going. I especially liked watching my hard penis with its thick black pubic hair plug into her pink vagina with its strawberry-blond thatch. It did fit like a glove and I do understand why men have sex with women. I am certain I never made Kathy orgasm, but she would put on a show as if she was having one, or two in a row. She was polite enough to fake them. I was polite enough not to tell her I knew she was faking them.

It took two more women to seal the deal, but I eventually stopped having sex with the opposite sex, with my healthy young penis. It took a very heterosexual, surly male actor in the drama department to help slow me down.

I was in college, senior year, fucking my way in and out of the green room of the Tufts Arena Theater, leaving a fictitious wake of women and a curling wave of men. I directed a play that I wrote and the lead actor of the play, Eliza, now a tough television producer, flew with me back to Boston from New York after winter break on People Express. She asked me, openly, and with great confidence, "During the run of the play, why didn't you make a pass at me?"

I thought it weirdly anachronistic that she was using the phrase "a pass."

I explained to her that I was bisexual and a bit confused and though I found her attractive, I did not want to put her in harm's way. Plus, I had already taken away the best years of someone else's life. She was not put off by this.

"Oh, we all do weird things. I had a three-way with my cousin. You know my cousin—"

I did. I had met him. In New York and on campus.

"So, we were all drunk and I was in bed with him and his girlfriend and then they started to fuck and so I joined in. We were laughing and talking about frogs. Someone was making frog noises during sex so we all started making frog noises. I fucked my cousin. That's just as bad."

I didn't think it was just as bad.

She was daring me to have sex with her. I did a few times, but it was less than spectacular. I knew that being poked in the ass by a male stranger with his big uncut dick in a restroom in Paris for just one minute was more exciting than any sex I would ever have with a woman. Once it really sunk into my resistant mind, I grew to the position with women where I just didn't have the erectile mojo any longer. I would eventually end up on all fours, eating pussy. I didn't hate it, but I was detached. It was a chore. Eliza didn't completely hate having bad sex with me, but I could tell she could tell I was not so into her. Our sexual relationship was short-lived.

Word got out that I was sometimes in bed with Eliza. Her on-again/off-again boyfriend, Hank, who eventually became a known comedic actor, mostly for his funny voices on *The Simpsons*, was not pleased. Though he was not dating Eliza at the time, he had a claim to many of the women in the drama department and I was literally eating into his territory. Word was that he was good in bed and had a large cock. He was an alpha male. I was an omega.

One of the democratic *esprit de corps* things about college theater is that everyone has to do everything so at the end of the run of a play you are assigned a cleanup duty. I played the hopeful love interest Vaska Pepel in Maxim Gorky's *The Lower Depths*, to medium acclaim, and after the show closed my job was to organize and put away the costumes. The costume shop was in a prefabricated building attached to the theater by a prefab hallway. I was organizing the shoes below the rack of distressed garments that did their best to sell the mood of nineteenth-century Russian flophouse despair when the heavy double doors whipped open. How he knew I was there I do not know. He had not even been in the show. I looked up at his furious face. It was Hank and I knew why he was angry and for a second I thought—How can he be mad at me for fooling around with Eliza? I barely fucked her. He hasn't touched her in months. What kind of world is this? What is he going to do to me? I feel like I'm in my bullying elementary school neighborhood except I can't go hide in my room that sometimes gets infested with flying ants, forcing me instead to pick some unsafe corner of my house.

Hank picked me up by my collar, threw me against the costume rack and said, "DECIDE!"

He dropped me to the floor, slammed the doors behind him and left me there to finish up with the shoes. Asshole. But I did decide. Eliza was the last woman I had sex with. Today, she is incredibly beautiful, with a narrow porcelain face and long dark hair. When I see her on Facebook, I am shocked that I was a person who was allowed to eat her out in addition to supplying her a lackluster insertion.

Years later, Adam worked on the popular network television show *Mad About You* and he got me an acting job as a co-star. I ran into Hank on set. He had a recurring role. He was very nice. He had no memory of the day he told me To Decide. At least, I did not bring it up. I was impressed with how well he treated the lowest-caste workers on the set. It felt like he was making amends for something. I felt very safe and warm around Hank. We had been in plays together, after all, and he only slammed me into a costume rack once.

Having made the decision, with the help of once-bullying, now-kind Hank, I became fully gay. Of course, it took more than

Hank. Other gay men I ran into had arrived at self-acceptance before I did, and they helped me enormously. They took me to bed and encouraged me to calm down and enjoy what I naturally wanted to enjoy. The drama department truly was dramatic. Then, once I started to go out to gay bars in Boston, the deal was sealed. There was a two-weekend sexual event with a fireman from Charlestown, when Charlestown was Charlestown, that was life changing. The way he fucked and the way he was so still and beautiful in his body, I wish I had a time machine. It was becoming easier for me to decide to become gay, not that I had any real choice other than to accept what I actually was.

Eventually, after all this gay turmoil and the failed relationships ahead, I was lucky to find Adam, a real man, if not in classic personality, definitely in physical structure, and truly, in so many solid ways.

I was not scheduled for a checkup with Dr. Hellman for another two months. Adam was being kind, but I could tell he was freaked out by my milk bottle distortion. He was still only caring from a distance. My penis may have reminded him that something awful could randomly happen to him, too, so he better not get too close.

Sometimes, a big trauma can send a person in a positive direction. College, with its drugs and sexual confusion, made it possible for me to give up thoughts of being straight and any kind of science career, a career that would have put me to sleep. Even though I finished with a biology degree, I was able to accept that I was gay and ultimately an actor-writer-musician-whatever. It turned out well, or at least it turned out that I felt alive.

This big bump in the penis road could also perhaps lead me to something that was self-accepting and viable. Maybe I would head in a different direction in my inner life and it would be even more enlivening than what I had lived so far. I could cast off the mortal coil while still a living mortal and experience heaven while still on earth. I had always held on too tightly to things anyway.

Janine Shackles, an older hospice nurse who put me up in her house during a long summer stock gig in the charming town of Sacketts Harbor, on Lake Ontario, once said to me over an ashtray, "When you get older, you lose everything." Then she listed the order of the destruction. Sight, looks, balance, hearing, family, friends, the body. I liked her. We used to chain smoke together and gossip like old school chums. By the end of the summer she was like my mother, and in the notes she would leave about dinnertime or the chances of me using the washing machine that day, she said she loved me. I loved her too.

We also talked deeply about life, death, the physical abuse she endured while married, my youthful ambitions and disappointments. As a caring Christian woman and a hospice nurse, she often spoke of how important religion was to those who are in their death throes. Janine had had her own near-death experience on an operating table. She had willed herself back inside her body so she could continue to raise her six children as a single mother. Janine told me, "I can assure you there is an afterlife. I saw it. I lived it. You can count on it."

I said, "That would be really nice."

"When I'm with my patients it gives them such comfort to know they are going back to God when they die. It's money in the bank for those who believe."

"What about the people who don't believe?"

She took a drag on her cigarette and wryly replied, "Well, they die, too."

·9·

THE MOUSE THAT DID NOT ROAR

Taint Good

Every few weeks I added a .5 cm screw-on metal disk to the AndroPenis stretcher. Like those Southeast Asian women with the neck rings, I was determined to lengthen my penis not only for beauty's sake but, even more importantly, for survival within the tribe. I toughed it out with my deformed milk bottle penis, hoping the AndroPenis would take care of not only its shape but also its size. In the AndroPenis manual it showed that stretching the penis made it longer and thicker. I obsessively looked at charts online showing how much increase in length and girth a man could expect from hours of the AndroPenis worn. Fantasy was essential. The stretcher did help, but incrementally. I was feeling impatient, but this was certainly better than signing up for the Nesbit, the operation that could straighten your penis but would also shorten it, something I would not ever do.

The Peyronie's book, the very one Dr. Hellman told me to stay away from, gleamed on my bedside table. I had to hold onto something. This book suggested the problem was mostly circulatory, that tight underwear was a terrible thing. It also stressed to stay away from alcohol, meat, and eggs, to increase turmeric ingestion, and of course, to buy all sorts of supplements. The only one I liked was L-Arginine. Promoting nitric oxide synthesis, it gave me full nighttime erections that did feel healthy for my situation.

I also did crotch tendon stretches, knees wide in second position, bent over and pressing my elbows outward, just above my knees bent at ninety degrees, holding for thirty seconds at a time. Another way to do this is to sit on the floor with the soles of your feet together as close to your crotch as possible, then lean over and use your elbows to press your knees downward toward the floor. This works just as well, but sitting is harder on the lower back than standing in second position so I stuck with the standing exercise. These stretches improved the blood flow and a feeling of weight and heft in my penis. Blood in the penis is pretty much everything. It brings in nutrients. It heals.

I purchased enormous baggy cotton boxer shorts by Calvin Klein, something I would suggest for anyone who likes to be aware of his penis and testicles, to feel his manhood unencumbered and weighty. They also have the side effect of allowing your scrotum to stretch, which was the last thing I needed. My testicles were already the size of GMO plums. It wasn't long before I could almost play hacky sack with my balls. As Myra Breckinridge from Gore Vidal's tart book said while eyeing the genitalia of a man, holding his disappointing penis and large testicles, "All potatoes and no meat." What a shame.

I had a curvature assessment already set up for January 21, but I knew I needed to be inspected sooner. After I was told yes, no, yes, no by the appointment maker, she was able to get me in two weeks earlier for the assessment. I had to get out of the woods with my tiny little mushroom head wobbling over my thick oak base. With nothing until then but the Peyronie's publication that I had been encouraged not to read as my guide, I maniacally stopped bananas, salt, and wine, lowered my meat and egg intake, and increased my consumption of almonds and apricots. (None of this necessary.) I continued with the warm wet heat, the AndroPenis stretcher, the crotch tendon stretching and trying to find a positive attitude. (These were helpful.)

We sold our Queens apartment and I was on the hunt for a rental in Manhattan. I found a good one, which gave me a place to put my focus that was not below my belt. Christmas came and I was happy to be fully caught up in household purchases for our new place in Midtown Manhattan: shelves, sofa, a television entertainment credenza and such. Soon, on January 7, I would be going back to the doctor with my sad penis. The holidays were rough. Adam and I did not have real sex. I would masturbate the mouse end of my penis while Adam rubbed other parts of me. I could not bear for him to touch the upper shaft, which had become about as thick as three pencils wrapped together. It would not get hard, really. It barely did anything except flop while I yanked it up and down and "thought of England," or any number of things you think of during a devastating war. I decided this was what our old age would probably look like anyway. I was so thankful Adam was by my side. He maintained a very steady attitude. He never let down his guard to show his true terror. At least not yet.

I always knew I did not possess the best penis on earth, but it was at least symmetrical. When you are a man, having sex with men is something that can happen often, especially if you are young and appealing. In my day, I was attractive on the upper end of the spectrum. I had the luck of being an A- in the real world, about a C+, or worse, in Hollywood. Not too tall, but not short, sharp features, but not too pointy, tight body but not too skinny, clearly muscled, full lips, greenish-brown eyes, lots of fun hair piled on top of my head—I could have plenty of sex, choosing from a pool of willing applicants.

I was never delusional about the status of my penis in this super-sized world. My earliest sex, at twelve, was with Peter, also twelve, from our little sexually experimenting boy group in the neighborhood. He had an enormous penis so I always felt like my penis was small. After years of other sexual encounters and reading about penis size, I learned that my penis was barely above average in length, which was six inches in heels. Additionally, I discovered that I had a thick penis for its length, so no one complained as they gobbled it orally or anally or, three times, vaginally. Lucky me, though I never would have been asked to be a porn star if I had happened to get in bed with someone who made those kinds of offers.

In my twenties, my store was always open. The Come On In and Browse sign was readable by anyone who was looking for my kind of merchandise. When they'd arrive at the register it was my choice whether or not to ring them up, and with a drawer full of cash from other satisfied customers there was no pressure for unwanted business. Though this extended metaphor makes it sound like I was whoring, I was not in the sense that I was never paid currency. But the desire to be paid attention to, to experience the excitement of hunting and being hunted, to have no shortage of sex whenever I wanted it, was its own economy. I fed off this, but carefully. Many men near my age, especially the ones a few years older, were becoming HIV positive, falling into AIDS and dying. It is not too much to repeat that contracting AIDS was a death sentence. I was terrified. Because I was a scientific sort and since the data showed that oral sex was low risk and unprotected anal sex was high risk, I proceeded accordingly.

I was often depressed as a teenager, in high school and during my early years of college. I hid behind bravado, academics, jaunts as an actor and staying as busy as possible. Because I had such a terrible time accepting my sexual orientation, when I would talk about the Gay Men's Health Crisis I would bitterly exclaim, "It would be the final joke if now, after all this bullshit of coming out, it ends up killing me." I felt so old and exhausted at twenty-two. But I still looked like I was twenty, so who was I to stay away from hotel lobbies, bushes, bars, bathrooms, green rooms, sand dunes and rest stops?

Even after Kathy, I would abstain for months at a time in the earliest of my twenties, trying to trick myself into heterosexuality. I had applied to medical school, and like Adam, who went to Wharton Business School in an attempt to ape the habits of a straight professional man, I had dreams of becoming successful, sexually normal and upper-middle class, a life of titanium and Teflon. But the over-compensator is exactly that. After I figured it out while bent over the sink in that Parisian bar bathroom at the end of my junior year abroad—and winced with a quick knowing that I was not going to make a great bottom—I had to get practical. After the howling, good sex over two weekends with the very masculine fireman from Charlestown, my senior year, I knew it was time to grow up and enjoy what I was meant to enjoy. I had an adulthood to face. My early desire was to become a straight movie star, but the fates were dragging me toward gay physician.

After I had safely returned to the grand ole U.S.A., the land of rational opportunity, I followed through in my senior year and applied to medical schools, took the MCATS and had my interviews. Being seriously considered to attend Tufts Medical School and New York Medical College was a great achievement considering my passion for actually becoming a physician only lasted seven months, during my sophomore year of college. Energy depleted on the physician front, I still had put in the four years of pre-medical requirements, so I had a natural inclination to follow this career non-story to its logical end.

In Paris, spring semester of my junior year, I met a woman from Colombia on a bus trip to central Europe. We sort of fell in love, or at least, she took an interest in my shenanigans and perhaps my American citizenship. I thought she was lovely and funny, warm and beautiful, but you know …

During winter break of my senior year, Otilia was visiting me and staying with my family in Ramsey, New Jersey, where my parents had moved two years prior. I was having unsuccessful sex with her in the small guest bedroom off the workshop in the basement, worse than it had been with Kathy and about as bad as it would soon be with Eliza. I had an appointment in Westchester for my medical school interview at New York Medical College, at the time rated 127 out of 127 medical schools in the country. The interview was ridiculous, with a faculty member in '80s cowboy boots preening like a sultan of Persia. It was mostly an informational sniff, this meeting, but he did ask me to ask him about himself, about being a doctor. I asked, "What is the worst dream you've ever had?"

He responded, "Something less personal."

I asked him something inane about the daily life of being a physician. He answered. His response was vapid and uninteresting but mostly, in tone, about his self-congratulatory ego and his cowboy boots. You can make key snap decisions when you are young without bloviating about the pros and cons in your mind. His ridiculous boots made it clear to me I would never become a doctor. I left.

When I returned to the car, my Colombian semi-girlfriend in her rabbit fur coat waiting inside, I realized I had forgotten my small black nubby vinyl portfolio with the all-around zipper, no handle, that contained I have no idea what, I do not remember. I did go back for it, mostly because there was no need to lose something. I got a little lost but found my way to the hallway where I had had my interview. The doctor in his cowboy boots had disappeared, off to wrestle diseased steer no doubt. I poked into the office next to the office where my interview had been held. There was a man there, an administrator. In those days, administrators appeared like secretaries to me, so I assumed, in my twisted, sexist way, that he was gay. I asked him if he could open the office next door to get my missing valise. He obliged. We went in. Then he got on his knees and sucked me off. He was ten years older than me. Bearded. Thankful for the opportunity. Clearly well-rehearsed. I wiped down, thanked him, and went back to the car with my nubby portfolio. Otilia and I drove back to New Jersey.

Feeling guilty about having wasted years of Kathy's life, the next day I told Otilia that I thought I might be bisexual (that gateway drug to homosexuality). She said she just didn't see it in me, that she had a little brother who had "this problem" and that her parents were working it out with a doctor to make sure he would get it taken care of. I had sex with Otilia, sort of. She had perfect light-brown skin, a thatch of straight black pubic hair and a completely tasty, perfectly shaped vagina, just like a small triangle. The hair did not go outside its lines. Her thighs were completely smooth. She had vulnerable dark eyes and a completely attractive overbite. We only spoke French to each other, which made us seem very romantic to others. She was the second of the three women with whom I had sex that included actual penetration. I was not very good at it with Otilia. I did not maintain an erection. My penis failed me. I was nothing but ashamed.

Otilia assured me in French that it was all okay. I thought in English that I was sick to death of being embarrassed about my limp penis when I was in bed with women, trying to make it all work. We both understood this was the end, that she and I were not going to get married or anything, that she would have to go back to Colombia, marry Alfonso, have children and continue to live the life of the daughter of a shoe manufacturer who often made business trips to Miami, which is exactly what she did.

Alfonso was nice. He had also been on our bus trip to Berlin, Prague and Vienna. He did not trust me, but we liked each other. Otilia was completely sexy, down in the basement guest room of my parents' house on Sherwood Drive in Ramsey, but my penile response to the bearded stranger in the small office of the medical school was much more affirmative. And it wasn't because of who he was but because of what nature set me up to enjoy. This thing, this young flesh of mine, was a pleasure machine, and I was someone who greatly needed pleasure. The results of the experiment were in. My penis, connected to all sorts of ideas and needs in my head that I did not want to understand, told me clearly what I wanted.

I lost touch with Otilia. She was deeply curious and alive. On a windy winter day in New York City, she looked up at the tall buildings of Rockefeller Center, wrapped her fur coat tightly around her chin and, making fun of all of it, said in mock upper-class British English, "Oh, Man-Hat-Ten." If I had been straight, I would have married her that day. Our children would have been completely international. Her skin never would have wrinkled. We would have always had fun together since she was so upbeat and curious. And her father would have paid for the whole thing.

A few months later, I had my desultory bed shame with Eliza, Hank pushed me up against the decision rack, the good sex continued with the random, hot fireman and others in Boston, and it was all over with my penis inside the ladies. It was not for me.

The best thing about having sex with women? The vulnerability. At least with the three women I had sex with. They looked right into my face and let down their guard. This was pleasing. My experience with men has been that they do not jump so quickly into openness. Plus, with women, you never have to compare your dick with theirs. Of course, they may be comparing your dick to so many others. But kindly enough, I never had to listen to any of that.

Now it was early January. This was the big day—my curvature assessment. I went at 4:00 and I updated my address, out of Queens and into Manhattan. No need for administrative problems. Putting things in order for one minute while entropy continuously tried to disorder my penis made me feel calm for the very short term. I settled down into the examination room in the basement. I was given the erection shot close to 5:00. I had the *Latin Inches* magazine again. This time I was more relaxed, able to stay hard, and I did not need a second shot. I am not necessarily drawn to men of a certain ethnicity—I like them all—but I do like many inches of penis blasting my retinas. It did the trick.

My nurse from the Slope, who had become so human to me that now we can get her a name—Regina—was funny and kind. She joked bashfully about her role in the clinic, calling herself a perv, chuckling over dispensing pornography. Dr. Hellman was calmer and more affable this time. In fact, he even seemed likeable. I did not want to show my panic over my incredibly shrinking penis. He would just blame me for being a Type A personality. I despise showing my fear outside the house. Dr. Hellman liked to be in charge and he did not like strong displays of emotion. I imagined he was not unlike the other pre-medical students I went to college with, who were mostly looking to get rich by tapping into a lucrative, reliable career. What was essential was to keep your head down, study your ass off, treat everyone else like the competition, and win. This does not make for the most open-hearted human beings. There are exceptions. I have met very few of these exceptions.

I was a shy child and suffered mightily in social situations as an elementary school student. This resulted in epic loneliness and a vague feeling of being defective. In addition to having to act more boy-like than was natural for me, by the fifth grade, I learned to ape an outgoing, party-fun personality that also included pleasing others at any cost. I assume I did this subtly so it was not too obvious, so that I would be included, maybe loved, maybe not ridiculed. I certainly was giving Dr. Hellman what he had ordered: compliance in the form of not showing distress. But effort made is only that and Dr. Hellman knew I was distressed, and he was guarded so as not to take on my pain.

I am very happy to not be a doctor. I was waitlisted for enrollment at Tufts Medical School and New York Medical College. I worked at Tufts Medical School for one day the summer between my last two years of college, which was the only time I used my biology degree professionally. No matter what, I would always have the memory of the impromptu blowjob in Valhalla by the talented administrator at New York Medical College, the usual way I use my biology. I could have made a fuss to actually matriculate into either of those schools, but I did not have the interest. I was called more to the stage, which became its own evil scientific experiment. I loved the logical study of science, in some ways, more than the chaos of creativity. I did not like so much the coolness science required in order to be practiced. I thoroughly hated having to be cool with a doctor when I was distressed in order to protect the doctor, to please the person, but I am flawed and built for harmony. My neural pathways have always controlled this behavior. I have worked, assiduously, in my middle age, to learn how to be hated without stress, to even enjoy not caring when barbs of loathing are shot in my direction.

I had written down questions to ask Dr. Hellman about the stuff I had read in the book that I was not supposed to read. Like many helpful books that tell you everything and maybe nothing at all, it had chapter headings that covered the main areas of concern for any condition from chemical to spiritual and beyond. Any appointment with the Grand Wizard of Peyronie's disease was a chance for me to gain new knowledge or to reconfirm old information. I did not ask him about the supplements he had already vetoed. But I had a new list.

I asked Dr. Hellman, "Are any of these pills useful? Pentoxifylline, Ubiquinol, L-Arginine, Trazodone and Glycine?"

"The L-Arginine won't hurt you. It increases blood flow."

"How about the Vacuum Erection Device, manual massage and applying heat using a hot wet cloth?"

"If the heat makes your penis feel better, fine. But that is all it will do. Don't massage your penis. We'll talk about the VED."

"What about Auxilium?"

"Useless."

"The book, and I know you hate the book, but the book said I have to watch my food intake. So what about these diet restrictions—Meat, eggs, cheese and wine?"

Dr. Hellman said, "It's all hogwash. Especially the supplements and the food advice. Throw that book away. Stay away from Trazodone. A friend of mine in Chicago uses L-Arginine. You can take that. It really won't hurt you."

"Okay. Thank you, doctor." I was relieved. Advice from a breathing being feels so much better than advice from a scary, overly informative book, even if Dr. Hellman was riled by my anxiety. After reading the entire book I should not have read, the only supplement that was of any use was L-Arginine. L-Arginine is an amino acid that is converted in the body into nitric oxide. Nitric oxide causes blood vessels to open wider for improved blood flow. I have found this to be true with L-Arginine and I recommend taking it before bed for anyone that wants a pretty ass-kicking nighttime erection. This fills the penis with healthy, healing blood. It also helps with daytime erections, though Korean red ginseng or Cialis takes the cake in the erection department for sexual encounters. I prefer Korean red ginseng. It does not give me headaches or stomach trouble. All the pharmaceuticals for erection pound at my skull, entice acid reflux, and sometimes even make me dizzy. I never combined any of these supplements and medications on the same day. This is very important, otherwise your blood pressure can greatly decrease, which is something you never want to happen. There was only one thing the book focused on that Dr. Hellman fully approved of. The VED, more commonly known around urology departments and online size queen clubs as the Vacuum Erection Device.

My penis, at this curvature consultation, was the most erect and plump I had seen it in a long time—the erection needle really does do the trick. I was large and in charge. I felt relieved that with some sort of aid I could actually have a penis that stiffened. I still had the bottlenecking, but it was much less constricted and definitely very hard. Dr. Hellman called this bottleneck shape distal tapering. He said that my problem no longer required stretching and straightening with the AndroPenis, but rather, a reckoning with the 3D nature of my distortion.

"I think you can stop using the AndroPenis. It won't do anything for a three-dimensional problem. It's time to head toward the VED."

Dr. Hellman handed me a prescription for the Vacuum Erection Device and the DVD that showed how it worked—quite a little package. He also gave me a prescription for Cialis. He said Cialis had the least amount of side effects, though I found, when I did use it, that the headaches were almost as bad as the ones I would get from Viagra or if someone were to hit me between the eyes with a cast iron skillet. Cialis was also very hard on my stomach.

"Call me in three months to let me know how the VED is working."

"Great. And can I talk to you about writing an article?"

"Sure."

Fun. People like having their portrait painted or an article or two in their favor. Dr. Hellman appeared flattered and calmer. I did want to write a simple article about penis treatment, but then it grew into this, this book.

I was relieved. Seeing my penis look so good lifted a huge scary load off my chest. I was ready to get that vacuum device, to plump up the front half of my penis. Cialis as needed. Continuance with the L-Arginine, but not on the same days as Cialis. Dr. Hellman said, holding out his hands like he was measuring a large fish, "If this is the Peyronie's spectrum, this is Don Cummings, here." He held his left hand still and moved in his right hand all the way to the left to make a small space on the very edge of the Peyronie's scale. In this fish story, I was a minnow.

He added, letting me know how lucky I was, "Some men get distortion in three planes."

I imagined those corkscrews. I felt so great that I went home, ordered the VED, got drunk with Mark, Drake and Robert, a gay Broadway business trio, one of them from Canada, smoked two cigarettes, felt awful from the celebration, and collapsed into bed.

My mood about my penis greatly improved. If my penis could become so plump and erect during a curvature assessment, even with the aid of an injection, that meant that my tissue was not entirely damaged and there was hope for the future. Distal tapering to be fixed with a VED? Dr. Hellman appeared very confident. I would prevail.

Even though Dr. Hellman had told me to stay off the online sites, I could not stop myself. When I was home during the day, Adam at work, I was lonely in this and needed to hear from others. On a Peyronie's forum site I posted about my success with my treatments, mostly because it was true, partly because I wanted to encourage others, and lastly because if it were in print, well, then it was confirmed and would solidify my future as a Peyronie's disease conqueror. I saw myself as being at the last hurdle. I thought—What's a little distal tapering when you have a vacuum pump, an optimistic physician and a penis that can, with help, really fill out? I would proclaim, online, my victories so far. I believed that staying the course, remaining positive, following doctor's orders and coming out online put me in the final stretch.

A fellow sufferer contacted me from the site, wanting to know more information. We chatted. He was very strong of will and impatient with the medical community. He worked at Rockefeller Center. Since his hard rock confidence was smashed, I have named him Mr. Rubble.

Mr. Rubble dated a much younger man and had a very demanding job. He was tall, very white and very Irish looking, another Northern European with a bent penis. Like many New Yorkers, he was slammed hard into careerism. He had little time to devote to the healing of his penis. Up to this point, I had been committed to four hours each day strapped into my penis stretcher, but I was a stay-at-homer and could afford this kind of time. Dr. Hellman said I could go about my day with the penis stretcher on. This may be true for someone with a large penis head, with a thick ridge to hold the AndroPenis in place. I am more of a rocket than a mushroom. My ridge is not huge. The plastic lasso that holds the AndroPenis in place can easily slip past my ridge, and then my penis simply pulls out of it, like a Yorkshire terrier pulling its head from its collar. For me, sitting in place while wearing the AndroPenis became necessary. An executive in one of the busy Rockefeller Plaza towers, unless hugely mushroomed at the tip, was not going to be able to run around all day.

Mr. Rubble and I met and talked three times. The first time was at a Starbucks across from my new Midtown apartment. We bought our tea and coffee. We were both shy about our penis afflictions. We did not blush, but the force field of the awareness of each other, with our vulnerabilities in our pants, diminished us publicly and kept us quiet.

I asked, "Do you think we can really talk about this here?"

He sipped his coffee and lifted his brow to telegraph that Starbucks was not safe territory.

"Let's go up to my apartment. You ready?" I asked.

That sort of sounded like a sex invitation. But we were two mid-life men with bent penises. Neither of us felt put upon or threatened. We crossed the busy street and took the elevator up to the safety of my fun rental in a white brick building on Eighth Avenue.

Mr. Rubble and I had already caught each other up on our treatments by chatting on the Peyronie's site. We sat on my new espresso-brown apartment-sized Crate & Barrel couch, the Petrie.

"I didn't like Dr. Hellman," he said.

"How come?"

"The office got on my nerves. I asked him about collagenase."

"But that hasn't come out yet." I wondered why he even asked the doctor about it.

"The treatments weren't doing anything for me." He sipped his coffee. His body was not shaking but it felt like if I had had his big suppressed energy, I would not have been able to contain it and would have been shaking like crazy.

"Yeah, but ... you have to keep going," I said. I was surprised. I thought Dr. Hellman was the only game in town and anyone would be happy to see him. Plus, Dr. Hellman always said that Verapamil treatments were not enough, that the stretcher was a very important component. I was ready to deal with my Peyronie's disease (which is really a condition, not a disease, it has been said) slow and steady. Mr. Rubble was in a hurry. I had had so many annoying allergies and stomach troubles in my life that I had learned it was best to stay calm and to ride things through with consistency, heading toward your positive health goals. Mr. Rubble wanted to get this thing taken care of in a swoop. Pity the man who does not suffer enough throughout his life. He is unprepared for the surprising inevitable.

"Did it work for you?" he asked.

"Yeah, I mean, it did. It's not perfect. I have this constriction and slight bend, still, on the left side. It started on the right, much higher up, but that went away. I'm sort of back to normal.

My penis is working. It was really bad the last few months. I was very upset about it. But I am getting straighter. I still have some distal tapering. The top is not as plump as the bottom, but it's getting better every day. It was really plump during my last curvature assessment. I'm optimistic. Dr. Hellman said I can stop with the AndroPenis, but I find if I do, I start to curve upward when I am erect, toward my navel, so I still use it. I also use a vacuum device to plump it out."

"Can you fuck your partner?"

"Yeah. Not always. The VED is helping. It depends on the day."

"I can't. I can't even look at it."

Mr. Rubble was completely disgusted with his penis. He looked like he would be happier if it were removed. I understood. I had a few late-night moments in the kitchen eyeing the carving knives. One quick slash and it would all be over. Mr. Rubble, clearly distressed and unhappy, was also oddly removed from the situation, like it was a problem to solve that someone else was having, not him.

"I didn't think to do anything else but go see Dr. Hellman," I said.

"Yeah, yeah, he's on all the sites. Yeah."

I said, "Well, he does seem a little nervous. He changed my appointment times a lot. And then he changed the treatment. I thought I had to go six more times, then not, then yes, but maybe I don't. I guess I don't. I guess I'm done."

"You're lucky."

I was very concerned for Mr. Rubble. He had better do something other than not like this doctor. I believed Dr. Hellman when he said that early intervention was essential.

"How often do you use the stretcher?" I asked.

"It doesn't stay on. I can't really do it at work. I do. If someone comes in for a meeting, I have to take it off."

"Yeah, it doesn't really stay on. I use it at home. Dr. Hellman said you can pee with it on. I tried. It goes all over the place."

"I never tried that. How long do you wear it?"

"I try to get in four hours a day."

"I'm lucky if I get an hour."

"You have to do it for as many hours as possible. That's the trick."

"I can't. My job. I can't."

It made me feel good to help someone else by at least listening to him. Poor, tall thing.

"But you say you can really have sex now?" he asked.

"Yes."

"Then there's some hope."

"Oh, yeah, there is," I said, very upbeat. I felt it and meant it. I was insistent.

It was lovely to not be completely alone with this affliction, but I was very concerned Mr. Rubble was not following doctor's orders, or anyone's orders, really. I also felt competitive, like I was doing my treatment better than he was, and felt ashamed that I was not entirely altruistic. But boys compete, and this was another real live person to swap stories with! I needed to give him more affirmation about his sexual future.

"I was really bent to one side. The right. I couldn't get it in. It really hurt. I was so depressed." I offered this information, again, in a kinder, even more vulnerable way as an entrée to talk about our feelings. He did not take the bait. Mr. Rubble had a master of the universe edge and nothing was going to slow him down.

At our second meeting, Mr. Rubble came right up to my apartment. He brought me tea. He told me he saw Dr. Hellman one more time, but it was such a waste. That nothing was helping. He got on the list for trials for a collagenase study. Collagenases are enzymes that break the peptide bonds in collagen, which is what scar tissue is made of. Mr. Rubble also, sneakily, made sure he was not in the control group but was getting the real thing. He was the kind of charming man who got what he wanted. Many studies with collagenase have shown that it is about as effective or less effective than Verapamil in softening scar tissue. Mr. Rubble was excited about the trial collagenase treatments.

He was taking charge.

"And if this doesn't work, I'm going to get a consultation for the Nesbit procedure."

Oh, man.

I would not recommend the Nesbit procedure for anyone. Remember, though, I am the tortoise and not the hare in the medical world. I have patience, and to this day I still wear the penis stretcher about an hour each weekday morning while I read the news, books, *The New Yorker*. There must be a cartoon in there somewhere. There are many brands like the AndroPenis and it is worth the time to research the one that may be best for you if you need such a thing. I am not an AndroPenis salesman. It is just the one my doctor recommended, and it helped.

Mr. Rubble had to get back to work. He was impatient with me. We said goodbye, for now. I do not think he liked me that much. But then, I was still worried too much about things like that. It was wanting to be liked that might have gotten me into this mess. The hard pounding of the guy down the street when I lived in Queens, when Adam was still in Los Angeles, still haunts me. Sure, I whacked him with my wand willingly, but I only did this because I needed the affirmation from someone, some closeness, something, or I would simply have stayed at home. Maybe watched a little television like a less needy American?

I harbor great ambivalence about those sexual encounters with Mr. Rough-and-Ready, in his leather chaps, his wrists tied to his bed posts. It was fun to take someone over, to give him the pleasure he wanted. Another very hung guy with large bottom needs. He was the last guy besides Adam who got my good straight penis. I will never know if fucking him hard, in the throat, in his hungry ass, stressed out my penis material. It may simply be coincidence that the Peyronie's disease showed up a year later. I may be building causality out of guilt. But I do know I do need sex. I do need closeness. I was always grateful Adam understood this and did not mind if I went out to find someone to supply it. I will never know exactly what caused my penis to bend, shrink and indent other than random misfortune. *We Tell Ourselves*

Stories in Order to Live, says Ms. Didion. But sometimes, we do not know how the real story will end because it never ends and then we still fall apart in so many ways. What of it, Joan?

·10·

PRISON WITHOUT ESCAPE

J it Forward

By March, my penis in its erect state consistently hardened into an upward tilt. Making positive proclamations on the Peyronie's chat site and emotionally supporting Mr. Rubble did not magically end my trouble. The VED, or time, had returned my penis to an almost uniform thickness. I no longer had a mousey fore-penis. I was very grateful. The VED was responsible for this plumping? Or just a natural evolution? Again, no control group, so who knows?

But the ring of constricting scar tissue that had separated the two halves had become tough and stubborn. It appeared to me that I was calcifying. The ring grabbed tight in the middle of my shaft, giving my penis an hourglass shape during erection that the VED could not mitigate. A long band of constriction formed dorsally, on top, the full length, which forced my penis into the tilted candy cane shape, toward my navel, when excited. So now, when erect, I had a penis that looked like an upside-down J with a thin girdle around the middle. You can picture it if you let yourself.

It was encouraging that Dr. Hellman had been correct about the distal tapering, which had greatly improved. I used the VED every day for fifteen minutes, as prescribed, usually at night before going to bed. The DVD and the instruction manual were clear. I lubricated my penis head and the inside of the tube so my skin would not stick to the plastic. I also lubed the gasket that rested against my pubic area. Keeping the pubic hair shaved at the top of the penis made for a better seal. This was Dr. Hellman's idea and not in the manual or on the DVD.

The penis tube of the VED is very long and wide. Modeled after a particular Brazilian, perhaps, it certainly gives you a goal. The brand I used was called ErecAid Esteem, which was also printed on the tube longwise. The M of esteem was six and one-eighth inches from the gasket that was creamed up and suctioned against my body. My goal was to slowly get the tip of my penis to fill up the tube to that M and to stay there. It took me about ten minutes to pump it up to that size from a non-excited state. Then I held it for five minutes. My penis always turned a deep noble purple. Sometimes, it would get so red under the ridge of the head that I thought maybe I had pumped too much and my skin had ripped open and blood was coming out. But no, when I released the pressure to inspect my penis, it was just discoloration. I knew if I got to that red-looking ring of blood that it was time to let in some air, to decrease the suction. There was a manual release button. I decreased the time to ten minutes each evening. It felt like enough.

Some men destroy their penises with vacuum pumps. If you over pump you can rip tissue inside your penis and then that section will not get hard during an erection. You can, if you dare, join a penis-pumping club and do this sort of mutilation. Your penis, if you get into a pumping craze, will get much larger and will look bigger when flaccid, but it will not ever get truly hard again. I do not suggest this.

I did not pump past six and one-half inches. Six and one-quarter inches was the longest I had ever been anyway. (Many studies have measured the average erect American penis at five and six-tenths inches. Like many men, I wish I had eight or nine.) The constricting hourglass ring and the contracting dorsal bands felt like they were turning into chitin, the substance that makes the shells of horseshoe crabs tough. My upside-down J with the girdle on, pointing toward my navel, felt like it had discovered the final shape of its disease. When it was erect, poking at my belly, I could only think of two words—Meat Hook. This penis healing journey had had its moments of promise, but then the stalled irregular shapes wore out my soul. This was going on forever. My patience was shot. My youth was over. Though happier that my thickness was mostly restored, I was still deformed. When I ejaculated, the semen did not even exit because of the curve. Orgasms had a tourniquet feel to them. I had to urinate to clear the path. I felt hopeless.

In my darker moments I understood why Spalding Gray, the solo writer-performer, threw himself off the Staten Island Ferry to drown in the harbor. He was brain-damaged from a car accident and decided upon a "creative suicide." I thought the best thing for me to do was to jump in front of a subway. For Adam to collect my life insurance money I would make sure it looked like an accident by leaving a banana peel on the platform. "He slipped. We all saw it."

Humor does save a man, even the clammiest old saw. I am not for dying. I am for living.

But it was depressing to think that my sex life was possibly over in the insertion department, that this new shape, so horrific and unnatural, had taken over for good. I had submitted to all the treatments at Dr. Hellman's office with the menacing poking needles, along with the endless hours of stretching and plumping my penis, only to face this daily deformed shape that was looking worse than ever. Yes, my penis was more uniform in thickness, but the candy cane between my legs was anything but sweet. I felt desperately hopeless. I often fantasized, in the shower, with the glass enclosure wrapped around me, about no longer being here, no longer having to face my downfall from middle age to ash. Sure, I could get an erection, but I could barely stand to look at it. It was disgusting. I could not easily or happily inject Adam's favorite spot with this hooked penis. If I were to jump on an app to find sex and show this thing off as it really was, I would be blocked by everyone. I hated myself. I identified so greatly with my wonderfully thick, straight penis for so many years, and now what? Who was I? If I could not have my original penis, I wanted to throw a fit. Since I did not have the energy to throw a fit, I grew more depressed. I was not, nor have I ever been, truly suicidal. But I encouraged time to speed up so death could fix everything. But was this the wine, which I was drinking like a sailor, talking? I thought the wine might be an enormous contributor to my going down so emotionally. I stopped drinking entirely. Coming from a family with a few addiction problems, I figured it could not hurt. But if I have to be honest, and I do, there was a big event that brought me to my boozy knees.

On the last day of winter, going into my second year with Peyronie's disease, I had a glass of wine and a hit of mild marijuana and went to the new local gay bar on 52nd Street, called Industry. It was a weeknight. I was looking for a distraction, to get out of the house. Nothing more. My intention was to return home to go to sleep. A very attractive man, tall, trim, in a colorful shirt with a fine suit and vest, with medium-brown skin and an amazing smile, started to flirt with me. I truly was in no mood for sex, but feeling so awful about my penis, I was glad for the attention. I asked him what he did for a living. He told me he was a clothing designer for Macy's. Eric, my first boyfriend, well-hung in the kitchen bathtub and all-around theatrical horse fucker, had worked for Federated Department Stores, which owned Macy's, as a freelance illustrator. I felt like I was in familiar territory. This current Macy's man in this bar bought me a drink. I had it. I insist he drugged it.

Within fifteen minutes, I had no sense of my own will, something that had never happened to me while drinking. Plus, after he bought me the one drink, he insisted I buy all the rest. A classic move. He asked me to go with him to his place, but first to buy some pot from someone in the bar that he knew. I said I didn't want any pot, that I could just go home and come right back with some. He insisted he wanted to buy it right then. Of course, I had to pay. I forked over forty bucks and he left. I waited, like a weird zombie without choice. He returned five minutes later with a small piece of foil, opened it up and showed me the tiny amount of marijuana inside. It was absurd. This guy was a crook. Pot planted in his pocket. But because I wanted his attention and because he was pawing at me like I was made out of Brad Pitt, and certainly because of something in that drink, I truly lost my self-protective clarity of mind. Roofied? I do think it was something like that. Perhaps a Quaalude? I will never know.

He said he lived on the Upper East Side. We jumped in a cab. But first he wanted to go to a bar downtown. We went. Second Avenue and Second Street. I figured out later it was because there was an ATM in the bar and he was able to watch me swipe and get my password. We had more drinks there. Which I paid for. Then we went into another cab and started to head north, to the East Side, apparently go to his place to have sex.

—Whatever. Get it over with.

In the cab, he would touch me a little then pull back. He worked me, and I was in such a haze that just a few animalistic brain cells were firing. Whatever was in the first drink he bought me made me feel very relaxed, too, so I did not feel endangered.

The cab skipped the Upper East Side and drove deep into the Bronx, University Heights. By then, due to whatever was going on with the drug, I had become completely helpless. I was led into a neighborhood bar/restaurant. I was deposited at a particular table with Sally Bowles cabaret chairs all around it. There were a few large men sitting with me who made it clear I was not to go anywhere. My handsome friend, still ever pleasant, still nice to me, wanted me to order more drinks. I did. He took my credit card to the bar, which I did not resist, returned to tell me they did not take credit, only debit. He also took my debit card. Then he disappeared with both cards.

Finally, I realized I was in extreme trouble. The thugs at the table were not physical with me. They were just keeping an eye. It was very strange to be with men who were not really doing anything but babysitting me, but the deal was they were threatening. They could tell I would not go anywhere without my credit and debit cards returned to me. They also could tell I was not in my right mind. It was then that I knew that this was a usual game the handsome man played: find a mark, drug him, drag him to this place in the Bronx, steal. I was thankful no one became violent.

I knew I had to do two things: get my cards back and get the hell out of there. I kept asking where the guy went. My calm managers kept telling me he would be right back.

"Give me my cards back. I want my cards."

"Just wait. Just wait," they said calmly, in their warm Atlantic Ocean accents. I could have just left, but since I was not in physical danger, I figured I would wait, see what was up. I asked for a cigarette so I could go smoke on the side of the building. On my way out, I fell off the side step onto the metal dungeon door that exists outside many city businesses, landing on my shoulder. I stood up, not feeling any pain. I smoked the cigarette and went back inside, and about thirty minutes later my date returned. He gave me back my credit and debit cards. He continued to behave like a complete gentleman in his nice suit. I glared at him to let him know what a horrible snake he was. I was no longer in peril and I knew exactly what had happened. The drug was wearing off and I was furious. I stuck the cards in my pocket and ran out the same door where I had fallen, into the late night. By some miracle, like in a movie or in a dream, a cab drove up. I hailed it, jumped in, and went back to Midtown. I was never so happy to see my L-shaped studio apartment in my life. Something like that had never happened to me before. I generally do not trust people. I usually read people correctly. This had been an enormous mistake and surprise.

Adam woke up and was terrified.

"Where were you?"

"Honey, I went to a bar. I really only wanted to get out of the apartment. Have a drink. I met a guy. He kidnapped me. I went willingly. I was out of my mind. I was in the Bronx. It was awful."

I cried.

Adam was fine. He did not judge. He was just very happy that I had returned home safely. I was violated and scared, ashamed and furious. He saw it and was relieved I was alive.

Then, basically sober, I called my bank and my credit card company and put a stop to everything. They were simply great. You know how corporations can feel heartless? Not that night.

The next morning, I slept until noon and talked on the phone with my close friend Cecilia, in California, who was going through a divorce because her husband wasn't fucking her.

I said, "Adam never touches me."

"Well of course that's why you went out looking for something else."

"I swear, I really wasn't looking. I was actually very tired. I just wanted to have one glass of wine and talk to someone, anyone at all."

I really had been very tired and was glad just to talk to someone in that new gay bar. But chaos happens and victims get victimized. Cecilia and I continued to talk for two hours. She helped me return to who I was, which was me, someone who does not go out to bars to end up in scary situations.

Ever self-protective, after that night of drugged kidnapping, I decided to quit using all inebriants. I could not have a penis problem and a substance problem. It was too much vulnerability in one body. Traumatized and confused, I did not completely figure it out for a long time that I had been drugged. It took me six months to really sort out what happened that night. At first it was easier to assume it was all my fault, that I just drank too much so all I had to do in the future was *not drink,* so I could feel like I had control over this victimization.

I had never assumed I was a public target in any way. I am street-smart so if something bad happens to me, I assume it is my fault. It was outside the understanding of my life that someone would do that to me.

With the help of many others in a group, I succeeded, immediately, in dumping all pot and booze. Though not a long-term twelve stepper, I was happy the group was there because I needed to be clear-headed for what was ahead of me. I cannot speak expertly about the twelve steps, but I can say, "It works if you work it." Ultimately, I felt so controlled by the rules that it was not for me, but it was a safe place to deposit myself for a while. The most enjoyable experience was being head of the talent committee for the holiday show. I thought I would make some friends. I mostly met shy folks with poor social skills, angry comics with no sense of loyalty, and a slew of nervous wrecks.

It appeared to me at that holiday party that psychological troubles were actually the precursor to alcoholism, not the other way around. Well-studied, addiction has multiple causes, some biologically based. I am no expert on this. After some time, I did not feel like the steppers were for me. The only interesting thought I had about AA while attending the tedious meetings was that it was a repetitive, circular program because addiction was also a never-ending circular ride. You get to the end of the steps and your sponsor asks you to start all over again or for you to help someone new to start from the very beginning. I figured this construction of AA that mirrored the closed endless loop of addiction made sense. I got on the ride. It lasted two years and three months. I have the three-month, one-year and two-year chips stored in a metal Fossil brand wallet box along with some Forever stamps, three guitar picks and some Canadian coins.

Glad for the cleanup, I happily exited AA, thinner and with a better memory. I found AA crushingly boring and loaded with enough unique lingo that one could easily label it a cult. They were insistent that if I was ever to leave the group I would surely die, or at best, would end up returning worse than ever. This is what they told everyone. I could not take them seriously. Lastly, there was the whole idea, promulgated with bullying gusto, that your own thoughts were a detriment and only the ideas of the founding fathers of AA would save you. This grated my everlasting original mind so entirely, I knew I would not last. A trip to the Dordogne, with its proximity to the Bordeaux wine region, cured me of my sobriety. These days, I drink very little without any trouble. I can tie one on, but I am not strong enough to become an alcoholic. Plus, I like to do too many other things. Doctors say no more than fourteen glasses of wine each week for adult men. So be it. Marijuana? Doctors shrug.

I returned to the Bronx with Adam on a weekend afternoon, ten days after the kidnapping incident. I wanted to see where I had ended up that tortured night so I could report it to the police. I found the place by a dim memory of the street name. The step where I fell. The name of the bar. The hill where the cab came barreling down to whisk me off to safety. I learned where I had been.

A few days later, I went to the precinct where the bar was located to file a report. The main room was loaded to the rafters with cardboard boxes with case files in them. It was a mess. It felt very 1970s, with high peeling ceilings and brown desks. The clerk introduced me to Detective Smith. The detective told me the way we would have to catch the guy who took advantage of me was for me to drive around with an officer in the evenings and to identify him. I said I was up for it.

"But I could call you anytime. Our schedule is that you are a certain priority and if there is an opening on a Saturday night, we could drive around all night looking for him."

By his warning tone, he was dissuading me to pursue my captor. Detective Smith was very successful in helping me lose interest in my victimizer, though he never stopped being warm and caring. He really was serving and protecting me, psychologically, after the fact.

While filling him in on the details, I described my captor as being young, handsome, most likely Dominican, and well-dressed, and I said that I was very surprised that he would be interested in me sexually. The detective responded, "You know, if something seems too good to be true, it usually is."

He had to take a call. I continued to fill out the police report with another officer. She was a game woman whose eyes lit up with the adrenaline rush of finally getting the chance to find out the answer to a question she had had for a very long time. She was African-American and beautifully put together and talked to me like we were old friends. She was warm and I got pulled right in. She asked me about Detective Smith, "Hey, do you think he's gay?"

"I don't know."

"He doesn't have a girlfriend. He goes out on Saturday nights and doesn't tell us where he's going. Sometimes he goes to Philadelphia. Everyone thinks he's gay. Do you?"

"I have no idea. He could be. You could ask him."

"No, I can't do that."

He was higher up the precinct food chain.

Detective Smith returned and sat across from me. He was flirty. Here we go. This made sense. He was about my age. My unconscious, somewhat racist psyche assumed that since I was white and he was black he might find me attractive, much like the assumption my mother exhibited as she flirted with the African-American justice of the peace at my brother's second wedding.

"You know," the detective said, "this is a bad precinct. These kids are just bad. I got into this to help, but you can't really help these kids. They end up in jail. That's their life."

His tone, again, was more informative than the information. The joyless ride and petty theft I endured was nothing compared to what else must have been going on in University Heights.

"So, I'll give you a call and we'll go out and look for this guy."

That sounded like a request for a date. What had my life become? —I'm either riding around with a perp who is pretending to be sexually interested in me or I am riding around with a cop who may be sexually interested in me? I was not going to pursue this any further. The giddy female officer kept eyeing me, like we had conspiratorially agreed that I would do my best to figure out the detective's sexual orientation and out him, nonverbally but cleverly, right in the middle of this mess of an office. I gave her a look—Sorry, that's not why I am here.

I said to the detective, "I'm just glad I made a report. I just wanted someone to know what happened. I wanted it to be official. Then, if this happens to someone else by this same guy, at least there will be a record."

Detective Smith turned to the snooping officer, "You got that all down?"

The police report she was doodling on did not look official. It was scratches on scrap paper.

"So, I will call you the next time we have someone available to drive around to look for this guy."

"Sure."

I was not encouraged. We both knew he would never call me, that we would never look for the guy. The detective was compassionate. Frankly, I think being so frank about my situation, my sexuality, I actually may have helped him to come out in the long run. But who the hell knows? I've had straight English teachers treat me warmly. I fell in love with a couple of them. Nothing ever happened. They were not gay or they were. I will never know. Really, it does not matter. I had deposited my tale of woe to the proper authorities, walked away with the case number that I could supply to my bank and credit card company, and called it an experience. All while being completely sober.

Trying to be positive while not drinking, I considered my upside-down J of a penis with the girdle on it—Maybe the Darwinian advantage of this erection, though smaller and strangely shaped, is that it's actually harder, as Adam has remarked? But still, diminished is diminished. Then I would think of Frida Kahlo's back and all she achieved while in agony. Did you know that Ingmar Bergman had constant diarrhea? Now you do. My penis had become stubbornly deformed, and though Adam continued to say, "It's okay. It's okay," I could tell that, as a bottom, he was missing his weekly love pounding. He went into survival mode, which in his family means shutting down and running backwards. It's not wrong, that behavior. Maybe it is preferable, how Adam takes care of things. He was someone who stayed on track and I did like that. Sometimes, I think psychotherapy that pushed people to open up and share was not necessarily necessary for society but was simply a tool of cultural warfare, a way for Freud to get pasty Austrians, Czechs and Germans to behave more like Galician Jews. Because I am Irish and Italian, the two cultures battling for my soul, I am probably projecting my own inner conflict here. I may also be grabbing at straws or using my upside-down J to try to hook the colorful plastic arms of something uniquely helpful in a random barrel of monkeys. Primates are clever, and we love to find a way to win a good game. But often the prize is nothing more than one rotten banana. On a good day.

·11·

THE PACIFIC THEATER

Waning Crescent

Soon after the detective and I did not search for the sexy criminal who kidnapped me, with my penis in its dramatically J-shaped state, Adam's father was finally sent off to the nursing home. He moved to Idaho, to the town of Sandpoint, in the panhandle near Canada, to live alone, away from his wife. Adam's sister, Hannah, still lived there. Bill had a few friends in the area since he had left the town not too long before. His Lewy body dementia had progressed to the point where it was truly impossible for him to be cared for by Carol. She decided to keep her house in Baltimore. I softened my stance against his family. Sometimes you do have to push someone out on the iceberg. An extra meeting with the geriatric social worker confirmed it. The time had come.

We all sent our favorite digital family photos of Bill from holidays and birthdays. Hannah of Idaho printed and framed, decorated and installed. Carol flew out with Bill and helped set him up in his new home. Just one last time, Bill would have to make a very confused attempt to take off his belt and shoes at the airport security checkpoint. Carol stayed for two weeks and planned to return to visit Bill in the summer. She flew back to

Baltimore and never saw him again.

Carol and Bill met in their twenties. He took care of her, financially, her entire adult life. Now she was letting him go off on his own, demented. Fine. I understood why. But I became afraid of what was in store for me, being in this family. Adam and I had met even later, when we were thirty-one. If there was no loyalty in this clan's DNA, what was I, a completely lapsed but loyal Catholic, doing bedding down with someone from such a harsh Protestant tribe, individualistic and self-serving to the end of their days? Shudder.

Adam worked in the home entertainment department of a big movie studio when I first met him, back when VHS was the way you had to watch movies at home, before cell phones, when Kurt Donald Cobain was still alive. I had just left behind tired, spent, noisy New York City, with my actor résumé full of showcases, summer stock productions and children's theater tours, hopeful of becoming a movie star-ish. Or of some change. Anything. New York had become nothing more than a six-soap-opera, six-musical town. There were days when I wished the helicopter from *Miss Saigon* would simply crash into the theater where *The Phantom of the Opera* was playing just to clear out some space. There was no work. I was sick of living in small apartments with roaches. The usual New-York-City-You-Are-A-Total-Shithole-and-I'm-No-Longer-a-Kid-and-I've-Had-Enough story.

Before I was fortunate enough to meet Adam, I had to get to the West Coast and then bang around for a few months. I drove across the country in a white Geo Prizm bought from my car salesman brother, Charlie of Mahwah, visiting pals along the way, blasting through the brush fire in Anza-Borrego before I arrived in San Diego to visit my cousins and then went north to Los Angeles. I moved into Lillian's guest house—she was an old lady widow in Brentwood my cousin Bernard knew from his intern days. Bernard had worked at UCLA on rotation after medical school and had taken care of Lillian's husband who was a polio victim. Physical therapy. Breathing machines. Lillian had a very generous brunch in my honor the day after I moved in. Bernard and his wife, Caitlin—she was the cousin who had come with me to meet Louis's father, the incest machine, a few years prior—invited Bernard's old friends from UCLA. One of them was a saucy gay person from the UCLA medical lab, Jim, who, like everyone else at the table, politely choked down Lillian's experimental Indian cuisine. It tasted like coriander, fish heads and burnt rubber. Jim asked Lillian, "What is this recipe?"

Lillian proudly replied, "It is my own invention. I think it could start a trend."

"Lillian, the only thing this is going to start is a compost heap."

I liked Jim immediately.

Upstanding Lillian, with her gnarled arthritic hands waving us away, took the joke as well as she could while we could not stop laughing, though we were doing our best to try. Jim invited me to a party that night. I was happy to join him since my cousins were leaving that day and I was to be completely alone, with no one but this strange old lady chef as my landlord.

The party was in a large house in Long Beach. There were drag queens performing for a charity cause. The floorshow was lip-synched and lame. I regretted having left New York. Maybe something could come of this night other than profound homesickness?

I met Ted, a party guest. He was manly with thinning hair. He had the standard face you are issued in Illinois. White Anglo, blue eyes, handsome, a small sparkle. He wore a medium-blue denim shirt that enhanced his eye color. He flirted directly. He was sure of what he was doing. We started to date, it felt like, at that party. Ted worked for American Express taking care of all the payments that came into a PO Box in Glendale. He was a solid citizen.

Ted's thick penis was two-toned, like a Guernsey cowhide. It looked like a vanilla-and-chocolate Dixie cup. Vitiligo, most likely, was the condition. He was obsessed with work and wanted to make a million dollars before he turned forty.

"Why?"

"Because then my father will know that I made it."

Ted's obsession with his father drove most of his actions. It was his internal eclipse. Every action fed into his need to be very wealthy, all else being a waste of time. Ted was ashamed of his penis and preferred that I didn't look at it. I had no problem with the look of it. It worked well. It stayed hard. It was larger than mine. He was good in bed, sort of. Kind of uptight, always a little outside the act. He needed to prove himself and would ask me to grade him on his performance. I told him he was great but would be even better if he wasn't always trying to be great. This was August. We carried on for a few months. His cowhide penis was enjoyable.

When I met Adam at the dinner our friends set up, in October, I already knew a lot about him. One of his best friends from Boston University, Cynthia, had married one of my best friends from Tufts, David. This was the connection. Adam had recently come out of the closet and needed a boyfriend. I needed friends since I was new to Los Angeles.

Adam was exceptionally nervous at dinner, hosted by another friend, gracious Susan, along with her husband, Dan, who both also went to college with Adam and Cynthia. Adam talked fast and loud and had an oily sheen on his sweet young face. Adam has the coloring of a gift store angel, with blue eyes that were once truly like zircons. People remarked on them all the time. I was confident I had his attention. His anxiety was off-putting. I thought he might calm down over time. I knew I had him when a joke I made succeeded—calling Burbank, in a disdainful voice, *Beurre Blanc*. It was a party of five, the fifth wheel being Hogan. Dan invited Hogan at the last minute, by mistake. Hogan was cute, with sharp features and silky hair. I thought Adam and Hogan were a couple. I was wrong. Hogan was straight and eventually sired two daughters.

Adam and I took a serious interest in each other. Meanwhile, back in Glendale, Ted with the bovine-colored penis was revealing his money mania with larger swirls of anxiety. It was all he could talk about. His father loomed large in our relationship. I loathed his father even though I had never met him. Adam lived closer to me, was more fun, was definitely more interested in me than Ted was, and was not, thankfully, working for a credit card company.

Adam and I had two dates, both in Santa Monica, where he lived. I was late for both. The first one was on Ocean Avenue at the Alligator Café, now defunct. He slurped down two martinis before I arrived, which was forty-five minutes after our set time. I had no understanding of Los Angeles traffic; plus, I was often late for things. He was much calmer than he had been at the dinner party—wore his work clothes, which were a suit and a pale-blue shirt—and we talked about everything. Europe mostly. Our mutual friends. We had a lot of overlap. He had lived in France, Sweden and Switzerland working for various groups and corporations during and after college. I am a big French nut, spent that chunk of student time in Paris, and loved Switzerland. Adam recalled we had met at David and Cynthia's wedding. I did not remember. I was there with meatloaf Billy. Adam kept staring into my eyes, letting me know that he was completely interested but that I had to make every single move. Fine, I could lead.

Our second date, I thought we were meeting at his apartment but we were supposed to meet at Baja Fresh on the Third Street Promenade in Santa Monica. By calling into answering machines and leaving messages and checking messages by payphone, we straightened it out and I met him at the Mexican chain. It was a completely enjoyable and delicious date. But fast. After, we went to his place and we sat across from each other. It was clear that we both wanted to rip off our clothes and get down to business. But I still had Ted around. I said to Adam, "I am dating someone but it is not working out. I want to fix that." I kissed Adam at his door as I left. We made a date for me to come over one night soon, when he would make me dinner.

I had always had a theory that dating two people at once meant neither one was really working out. When you have two, you have none. I decided to clear out Ted very quickly. He could not have cared less when I broke up with him. He seemed relieved to not have to break up with me. Ted could go figure out how to please or never please his father. I was done with him. He was done with me. I never saw his two-toned penis or him again.

I went on my third date with Adam. At his apartment.

Adam made me homemade clam sauce. And the rest took care of itself. He wasn't as good at sex as Ted or as a lot of other men I had been with up until that night. He was so new at it. It was difficult for him to know what to do. Pulling back from him when we were on the pullout futon couch, with its dark purple and blue paisley canvas cover, making out, I was troubled by his inability to head toward abandonment while being sexually physical. But he learned. From me, and I am certain, years later, from others, but he was never going to be Italian about it.

We dated for fourteen months, endured the Northridge earthquake naked, grabbing onto each other, screaming in a doorway as the framed pictures flew off the shelves, broke up once because he could not commit, reconnected within ten days—I was inspired to call him after renting and watching *The War of the Roses*—fell more in love, moved into a two-bedroom in Santa Monica together, not far from his old place, and began our committed domestic relationship. You just witnessed the montage.

I was very puritanical from my mid-twenties to early thirties. Because of my bad drug experience in college, I barely touched any inebriants, not even marijuana. I hardly drank. I certainly did not smoke cigarettes. I was old-fashioned and monogamous. Additionally, if I was having any emotional issues with Adam, it affected me sexually. If I was mad at him, I could not get a boner. I was like a girl who stayed dry if her husband forgot their anniversary. I needed to feel safe with Adam. Perhaps this was the most emotionally healthy period of time in my life. I never self-medicated. I faced things head-on. I remarked that it may have been womanly of me to be so attuned to my feelings, but I was very happy that my emotional life and my sex life were intertwined. If Adam and I could work something out after a fight, I would end up feeling safe and the sex would be great.

We were still so young. I was afraid and lonely, trying to

succeed in the harsh business of show in a far-flung city without decent public transportation. Adam had so little relationship experience that he made mistakes, in my estimation, at a rate that made me question whether this duo we had become was workable at all. We were living together, with mixed reviews, with his two dirty cats, five blocks from the beach, sorting it out, clumsily, angrily, lovingly, our moods changing all the time. In winter, we could hear the ocean waves outside our window. It was romantic. It was also somewhat unbearable.

The early problem I had with Adam was that he came from a family that did not understand intimacy, as I have repeated too many times already. His parents knew nothing of each other's desires or needs, yet cohabitated. Adam's natural response to stress was to remove himself from people. He was happy to have fun with me, but any trouble and he would get angry. He would insist that I caused every problem. It would take days to resolve things, mostly with me being dogged, wearing him down.

There was an even bigger problem. Adam was very competitive and needed a lot of public approval. He was embarrassed that I was an actor with very few filters. He did not like how I interacted with people in public. If I decided to dance in a silly manner, he would die of shame. If I showed too much emotion, the looks he would give me were withering, the barbs sharp.

Adam did not fight with me in private because he did not have the skillset. He felt powerless at home so he compensated by fighting dirty in public. It was nothing for him to turn toward me after a few drinks, in front of his old college friends, and put me down brutally. These were the fights of our first ten years. He did not get what he wanted, which was for me to behave properly according to his preconceived notions that included not bothering him with my emotional crap while he watched television. He would retaliate in public by putting me down. I would get furious and we would then fight about it for a week, television off, me fuming.

It was not constant. We were both busy and had other things to do than to not get along with each other. I did not feel battered, exactly. The bad moments were quick. A look here. A stab there. A less needy person would have left him immediately. Hard resentment started to form the foundation of our partnership, not unlike in his parents' marriage. I felt the need to release some pressure.

When Adam and I were both thirty-four years old, in the third year of our relationship, I came home and asked him to sit because I needed to talk. This was the day of the sexually-opening-it-up reckoning, when it was all made possible. On two of the caned chairs of the dining set purchased from a country house in Great Barrington, originally owned by the family of his old friend, Susan, the woman who threw our first dinner party together, with a darkly stained pine table from Ikea in front of us, I asked him, "Would it be okay if we opened up the relationship?"

I was still being approached for sex by good-looking men and that very week had received tasty offers I did not want to refuse. I wanted to feel appreciated by others while Adam was disapproving of me. Adam, who never stopped talking about me being his first and only boyfriend, felt that he had missed a big chunk of early, gay, slutty life. He was envious of me for doing something he never did, which was have sex with men all over the place during my teen years and into my twenties. Not my fault, but I did see his problem. How could you be a gay man and really only have sex with one guy? Especially if that one guy was only me? I'm fine. But I'm not that fine.

I figured if we opened up the relationship, I could go have some fun, get some positive energy from some enjoyable men, which I was itching to do, and he could take care of those missing years and stop resenting me for, well, everything.

And we did.

And it was not a problem.

There were three rules. No repeats. (I broke that rule a few times.) No relationships with anyone else. (No problem. People are too difficult.) And Don't Ask, Don't Tell. (Simple.)

The rare romp with someone I met at the gym, happy ending

massages, occasional online hunting and out-of-town actions were all easy to pull off. Not much more. I did not want to love anyone else. Neither did Adam. I did not hear much about what he ended up pursuing outside of our relationship and I did not care. In fact, I was relieved that he did what he needed to do, that maybe he would not feel so trapped by me and then, perhaps, he would be easier on me in public. It did not work out that specifically, but it was a great pressure release for both of us. And Adam got better in bed.

In the second year of our relationship, a year before we opened it up, we went camping, alone, in Sequoia National Park. We were talking about our extended families.

"My Aunt Rita is on welfare. Always has been. She's alone in a senior citizen subsidized housing situation in New Jersey between a local highway and a parkway off-ramp."

Adam replied, "My Uncle Steven had a sailboat and once, we sailed from New York to Martha's Vineyard."

"I feel bad for my Aunt Rita."

"I wanted to be like my Uncle Steven."

From his behavior and tone, I did not get any sense that Adam cared at all about his Uncle Steven, whereas I was overly caring about a great aunt who really never did much for me. She just sat there, basically depressed, in the family.

I was very afraid that Adam cared about no one at all. There was no need for me to have such compassion for my great aunt, I imagine. She really did nothing in her life but present herself at holidays. But to like an uncle only for his boat or his swagger? Maybe I had made a huge mistake moving in with this cold, calculating creature. Or maybe I was a sap for caring about my Aunt Rita. Or maybe I was in my early thirties, financially unstable, and basically pushed into a relationship with this man by a bunch of his college friends and my one friend who married into the group, and it was too good a setup to leave. My love for Adam the first ten years came and went. I knew he felt the same way about me. He would often turn to me and say, "The only reason we stay together is because neither one of us can find anyone better."

It always stung. I sometimes agreed, though. Occasionally, the fights were so mean and bitter I would swear I was going to leave, and then ... old man inertia would kick in or my mother would call and respond to my grievances, "You think the next one is going to be any better? Believe me, he won't."

Unlike with Adam, though, as harsh as my mother could be, I could always feel her warmth.

In the middle of April, a little over a year after I discovered I had Peyronie's disease, three months after my last visit, a few weeks after I had been kidnapped to the Bronx, I went in with my newly-shaped upside-down girdled J to have a checkup and to talk to Dr. Hellman. My constricted, J-curved penis felt like it was definitely hardening into its new shape. I was happy that the wobbly-headed small upper shaft had fattened up. But to be so deformed, so constricted and curved toward my belly, and so upset and without hope—something had to be done.

Dr. Hellman, who, just a few months ago, had given me the fish hand signal that I was in the shallow end of the Peyronie's disease pool, said that this was a very rare event, that after getting so much better, it was unusual that things would suddenly turn so much worse. "This usually only occurs in young men in their twenties who get Peyronie's."

Ay, me. The only thing about me that is possibly like a young man in his twenties is my disease? I signed up for another curvature assessment.

By April 15 (Tax Day), a few days later, I had temporarily escaped trying to reconcile the brutal statements of my adulthood and was thinking about the ease of childhood with its dreams and future fantasies. Something about having no control over your body—it becoming its own monster—was quite exciting. I used to think there was something incredibly sexy about being a werewolf—to become so animalistic and to have no control over it. Could this J, this rhino horn penis, be my version? I had to reframe this horror movie. I needed to outrun my distress. My penis was harder now. This was pressure-flow mechanics. The same amount of blood was going into a smaller space. I was more solid when erect, as Adam had noticed. So here I had this rhino horn. Why not enjoy this thing that promised tough, curved insertions? I was tapping into aggression to displace the depression. I even used it in this new way. It required a certain position. Certainly, I had to be on top and in charge with Adam. I did that. It meant holding Adam's legs in an exact position, very high up, that allowed for me to fit inside. I did the best I could, but it was awkward and my penis was still very ugly. My beautiful cock had become a crescent. Penises come in all shapes and sizes, but all I had really wanted ever since I was young was a very straight, thick, long baton. I once had two out of three.

When I was twelve and many of the other boys in my neighborhood were twelve, we started to get curious about what was happening to our bodies. We often played the fainting game where you pant deeply for a count of sixty, hold the last breath, and then have someone squeeze you around your solar plexus so you pass out. I remember getting a strong metallic taste in my mouth. Perhaps from a buildup of the carbon dioxide? I can taste it now. But the fun bonus game we would play whenever someone was passed out and vulnerable was called, "Hey—put your dick in his mouth!"

We did this. There were about five of us. It would not have been so creepy if among the five there had not been two brothers: me and Charlie. For the most part, my brother and I avoided getting near each other's penises, and the one or two times it did happen, to no great end or any enjoyment, we said to each other, "Let's make sure that never happens again." It never did. This is not a story of incest, but at twelve, there was a free-for-all going on and almost anything could happen. It was mostly playful, like boys figuring out the most fun thing to do with their boxes of Legos. The best part, the absolute best, was you could play this game, this fainting game with the penis in a mouth, alone too, with the kid with the biggest penis who loved to have his penis worked on. And there I found myself. At twelve.

Peter was greatly developed for his age, with an eight-inch shaft thick as a baby's arm and an underlying urethra you could drive Volvos through, striped by a few lovely strong veins, all encased in completely soft skin. We fooled around for years. I would not mind if he came over right now. A smell memory hits me as I write this. The only thing is, when you are not even close to a solid six inches yet, without pubic hair, and you are dealing with a whopping thick "eight" with all the trimmings at the tender age of twelve, you feel you will always come up short. Later in life, after sexually sacking all sorts of men in all sorts of places, I did see, by comparison, that I was pretty much average in length, decent in girth. That would have been bad (or good) enough to know. But to have a younger period when I felt vastly miniscule compared to what I was handling—it had the effect of making me always want to "measure up" and reach for greater heights and widths within myself. Boys these days, watching all the online porn with the ten inchers in starring roles, must all feel like gerbils.

My penis being this size became a job, ultimately, of acceptance, because I knew that working on my member in some mechanical way to increase its size would probably hurt it. Peter was huge. I was not. Others were average to small and they experienced me as if I was large. Large, at least in the mind, feels better. I have not met a man who would not agree. Though I told this to a bear of a man I know with a very large penis and he said, "Men with large penises don't think about that."

I believe he is in the minority of men with large penises, based on many online requests that clearly spell out, "Hung 4 Hung."

Peter and I never came close to intimacy. It was always alienated sex. For him, it was better than masturbation, nothing more. For me, it fueled the fire of sexual frustration since we never got the heat going frequently enough. When we did get together there was great arousal, but it was tinged with resentment, as neither of us liked the other very much in real life. He was hyper and only thought about himself. I was bookish and wanting. I guess I was asking a lot from someone who often slathered peanut butter on his dick so his dog could lick it off. He eventually married and had a few children and turned hard right in his politics. He was the only male sex partner in my neighborhood available to me as a teen. There was no chance we would ever fall in love with each other. He was too energetic and annoying. And straight? No one, really, has ever had a penis that I liked more than his. It became, in my mind, the Ur-Penis. I hope his is still working well.

On April 27, I went in for another curvature assessment for plaque. Dr. Hellman had moved his office up to the third floor. Jarring, but I could take the change. It was very quiet and there was a view of trees. It took a long time for them to call me in. They could not find my chart. They eventually found it or started a new one. I was so sick of their disorganization, but in my acceptance stage or whatever I was in with my rhino horn penis, I just had to go with it. Plus, I had come this far with these people and it did feel like they were the only game in town. On the Peyronie's chat sites, most guys talked about visiting one or another doctor who would say, "There's nothing you can do about it," and then send them home to twist and curve into the night. Hoping that it would resolve itself, because sometimes it does, these doctors were wary of treating something as tender as the penis, with its layers of easily scarred tissues. I am not one to hope nature will deal me good cards. If I ever get cancer, I'll irradiate my whole neighborhood and take chemo baths with my eyes open.

When I was four years old, I was stung by a bee and came into the house crying. My parents patched me up and I went back outside to play. Twenty minutes later I was scratching at the screen door, unable to breathe. My parents scooped me up and rushed me to the hospital, and I was given shots of Benadryl. I had stopped breathing long enough that I went into a coma. Or at least my mother calls it a coma. I did lose twenty-four hours.

My father said I was never the same. He perceived me as always being afraid of the world after that. My experience was that I was correctly being vigilant.

At the penis assessment, I brought in a stash of magazines. I donated two to the office and used a new issue of *Inches* for myself. Regina gave me the get-it-up-shot. I did what I could with *Inches* in hand. Then Dr. Scavone, the not-often-seen doctor, came in. He asked me some questions that brought me down. I asked him to leave so I could get things up again. He exited. I scrambled into the porn and then he returned to measure the curve with his hinged ruler, to feel the plaque and perform the ultrasound. He told me I had good blood flow. Everyone was always impressed with my blood flow. I did not think it was necessary to do this curvature assessment since what I said it was, it was: a candy cane toward my belly with a ring of constriction. I knew I would need more treatments. I signed up for six.

I waited fifteen minutes. Regina checked on me to make sure my erection had slinked down. I said, "It's an acorn now."

Regina laughed. I went home.

·12·

LOSING OSAMA BIN LADEN AND ADAM LECOMPTE WARING

A Mixed Bag

I had six more Verapamil treatments between early May and mid-July. The first treatment was the day after Osama Bin Laden was killed. Like everyone, I was jubilant the day Obama killed Osama, but I was even more impressed by how the president kept his complete cool during the whole operation. He even played the card game Spades while the planned assassination went down. All Obama's speeches about the success of the rubout were exceptionally low-key. If I had killed that terrorist, I would have been jumping up and down like Carol Burnett as Eunice, screaming, "I killed him! I killed him! I KEEEIIIILLLLEDD HIM!" If Obama, under such Jupiter's atmosphere-sized pressure, could remain so calm, perhaps I could go into the next round of penis injections with some equanimity.

I asked the male nurse, John, while he was giving me the first treatment in this new round of six, about the large mass of plaque on the top of my shaft, which was grabbing on like a starfish, trying to suck the meat out of a mussel but failing, "I guess I'm here the second time because this portion of scar tissue was probably forming—but it was in the early stage and now it's gotten worse ...?"

John said, "Yeah. That's a good deduction."

I often jump on top of things too quickly, like when I make dinner reservations before everyone is confirmed for the date. It is hard to know the perfect moment to pull the trigger. Had I not jumped on my treatment right away, the spring before, maybe worse things would have befallen me. I took care of it quickly, but all the scar tissue had not yet come to the table.

A week later I had an appointment to call Dr. Hellman. We spoke and he repeated that my case was highly unusual, that a second occurrence usually only happens to younger men in their twenties and thirties. I had already decided in my mind, and with John, that this second plaque had been forming and just hadn't coalesced until now. Dr. Hellman told me to resume the traction device, the AndroPenis, three to four hours each day and then he assured me, "Since the Verapamil treatments worked so well last time, they will probably work well this time, too."

I emailed Adam to give him the news with a postscript I was appending to almost all my updates—*Let us never forget. I have good blood flow.*

The Sunday evening a week before Obama killed Osama, Adam's father, Bill, fell, broke a hip and lay unconscious on his Sandpoint, Idaho assisted living bedroom floor. The following morning, he went into surgery. Adam's brother-in-law, an orthopedist, performed the operation. The surgery was successful, but Bill did not come out of anesthesia. He remained unconscious for one week. The Sunday night before Obama killed Osama, Adam's father died. Like Michael Jackson's death by injected drugs eclipsing Farah Fawcett's death by anus cancer, Bill's passing was dimly lit. There was relief in Adam's family. Understandably. They had been through enough. This sad situation, however, reignited my terror. Bill only lasted six weeks in assisted living. Chances are he could have dropped from a stroke at any time and this could have happened anywhere. But he was abandoned and alone. No matter how hard it had been to care for him or how difficult a family member he had always been, his exile forced his death. Like the hammer-wielding carpenter, because of his predilection, sees every problem as a nail, to me, every human movement is a reminder that I can easily be forgotten.

Adam's father's death occurred just two weeks before my second treatment. The very quiet day I went in, Nurse John said everyone else was at a urology convention. You can just imagine them all at some hotel in Vegas around a pool shaped like a kidney. A new-to-me nurse, Nancy, helped John with the shot to numb my penis. John left. Nancy stuck around for a bit.

"I'm a life coach," she said.

I have always liked life coaches. They have all the positive spin of a therapist without any desire to stir up the mucky dark crap that we all try to run away from. Of course, your dark crap will stop you in your tracks even with the most positive energy trying to wend you onto a successful path. But I do crave optimism, and when I find someone who has decided upon the optimistic life, I let go of all boundaries and give the not-so-subtle energy request—Gimme it. That! I want it! In Spades! (Isn't Obama handsome? The game of Spades he was playing reminded me.)

Nancy, the penis-numbing life coach, felt like my immediate pal. I headed toward intimacy. "My Grandpa Cummings blamed the war for his bent finger when it was most likely from Dupuytren's contracture. Or let's face it, it could have been from an accident at the carpet factory in Yonkers where he used to work. Stories. You never know."

Nancy said, "My father has an obvious lumpy stomach tumor under his skin and he tells his grandkids that it's from a bullet."

This closeness to pretty Nancy, an upbeat blonde if there ever was one, kept me warm and ready for more interaction.

"This Peyronie's makes me feel like I am having my first old man disease. Like I'm in decline."

I know I had said this before to others, but it was good to test everyone. See if the information held.

"Oh no! People who are in their twenties get it. You should not feel that way."

I said with a knowing face, "Oh, then just because I think something, it is not necessarily true?"

Nancy laughed. John performed the treatment, puncturing my plaque with about thirty needle holes. Nancy staunched the bleeding by applying pressure. We did not talk much while she was squeezing my penis.

The walk home across the park was very green and drizzly. I was half-filled with hope. Only two treatments in and my penis was getting chubbier and straighter. The upside-down J was becoming just a bend, not a curve over. Five days after this treatment, my penis became more curved again, and it was still dented around the middle, but less so than before.

Adam and I went to the Idaho panhandle for his father's funeral. Bill was a Quaker and meetinghouses throw simple get-togethers. Lots of covered dishes and pies were brought over. The Friends posted a sign on a clunky, square, stuffed, ochre-and-sage striped velour chair that said, *Bill's Favorite Seat*. Adam's mother was tired and relieved that her failing husband had come to his end, but grief did visit. We were in the car driving her back to the rental house we were all sharing and she started sobbing, "I realized that he did love me. He did. Now I know it. He loved me. How he loved me."

Sometimes it takes a death. Admittedly, he was not a demonstrative man and his attraction to women was always in question. She must be forgiven for treating him so coldly, sending him off to die in Idaho. If possible. Sure. I never understand why people stick around if they do not feel any love. The money, I guess. The house, certainly. The kids, so often. Inertia. It's a law of physics and the bane of households.

A week later, back in New York City, Adam was treating me like a stranger. Having his father, someone he did not like very much, disappear, must have been riling him up in a few emotional directions. It was no problem for me to give him all the space and time he needed, but underneath his grieving-celebrating distance was a chilly disdain toward me. My penis was on the mend. It really felt like the worst was over. Being the one who brings up the emotional questions, I asked him, "What's going on?"

"I want to break up with you."

This was not a surprise. This was the latest iteration of his resentment toward me for not behaving or doing what was proper, in his mind. I was feeling stronger, more penis-healed, and out came his ax. He must have felt I was ready to handle it.

In the early years, Adam's judgment was meted out because he did not like the clothes I wore or because I did not watch enough television. Most of our first decade together I embarrassed Adam because I was, as mentioned, demonstrative at parties with friends. I did have a mouth on me. I usually was in charge of that mouth, but sometimes I blew it. I have never liked small talk. We did lose contact with one of Adam's friends who I did not find interesting at first. During an excessively long-winded catch-up lunch—this mild Midge had been living in Hong Kong—I wanted to bang my head on the table from the numbing chatter. Adam had all these business friends. They stuck to conversation templates. Most of them were just trying to fit into corporate culture or to behave like proper adults. I wanted freedom.

The conversation turned to family. How this one or that one was doing. I was completely left out, uninterested in the yammering and angry that this lunch did not have an ounce of spontaneity or a whiff of ever ending. When the subject of Midge's mother came up, I distantly mentioned something about fucking her, clearly something I had never done since I had never even met the woman. It was a lame attempt to change the tone, to offer up my comedic nihilism as a gift to some open door, to show that I was ready for anything else at all. I was also angry and wanted to strongly telegraph that I was tired of being excluded in what was an endlessly boring conversation about people I did not know.

The failed joke, if you could even call it that, was a disaster and we were never invited with all the other reindeer friends to join the reindeer games up at Midge's swank ski house in

Whistler. Fuck Canada, anyway, right? It took Midge a long time to forgive me. I did apologize years later, and we did become thick like Irish-American thieves, all drunk at her sister's wedding. Celtic Catholics have been known to forgive, especially after a night of sodden sentimentality.

As the years wore on the breakup reasons Adam shook in my face were more over things like, "We don't have enough in common," or "You don't make enough money," the usual garbage you read about in lifestyle articles of the conventional. Adam wanted what he wanted and I wanted to be who I was. This often had the strange effect of infuriating him. I always had the strange reaction to stick around, because in my birth family, I was used to being tolerated, at best, occasionally highly appreciated, but mostly experienced as a strange annoyance that was loved anyway.

After Adam told me he wanted to break up with me, his father's donated corpse barely dissected at the nearby medical school, I grew cold and distant to match his mood. I flatly asked, "Why?"

Adam said, "The obvious reason is because you don't have a job."

This was nothing new. I actually did pull in a tiny amount of money from different freelance businesses, managed our Los Angeles rental property, and had made plenty of money in the past that had made the future all possible. Additionally, I have the accounting gene so nothing is ever wasted and money is always growing. In fact, my unconventional life was outwardly very conventional. While a creative back in my thirties, I had to admit—As I noisily rebelled against my parents, I silently became them.

People have their money problems, which are really fear problems latching onto money problems. Adam and I both grew up middle class, in families that behaved like they had lived during a three-hundred-year depression.

I intuitively felt Adam's breakup energy coming during the death and funeral of his father and I figured I would do a brother a solid and give him some room in case I was simply being paranoid. He was resenting me. —What else is new? Let it slide. Surely I had resented him for not giving me enough physical attention over the years, for being a stick in the mud when things got loose and fun, for forgetting all sorts of important things, like turning off the burner on the stove before he went to work or picking up red wine vinegar. If he wanted to distance himself from me during this stressful time of his father's death, I imagined it was because he was panicking over his own mortality. There was some truth to that, I was certain. I did not take it too seriously, at first. Plus, fuck it. If he wanted to break up with me, maybe I could survive out on the relationship open market.

"So, what's the deal, Adam?"

"I want to break up, but I feel trapped. With the Peyronie's, I feel it would be cruel to leave you. I would never forgive myself."

Funny, I thought—If he left, I'd live. I might have to date a dwarf or a bearded lady, but I can love and be loved, still. No big deal. My penis was really improving.

—So fine. Let's end it. Sure.

Furthermore—Fuck him and his pettiness. I'm still cute. People of another caliber still want me and I can become a bottom to some older gentleman with a few pounds on him if necessary. Career trouble? Always. Sex and love trouble? Not usually. Even with my rearranged penis, I still had some life in me. I was furious at Adam for pulling away from me during a time when we were both in distress. I looked at our furniture. I divided up the stuff in my head. I calculated the money even more swiftly. I would survive. It would be less enjoyable. But I could handle a breakup. I could go back to Los Angeles and work in television production counting the beans like I used to, maybe attempt a return to the small screen of television acting, and hang out with my more relaxed, funny friends. I'd had enough.

I said, "Let me know when you're done hating me. I would really rather leave when we are at least neutral."

Adam stared at me, scared and nasty all at once, saying nothing. It was the silence of Adam, the way he did not express himself, that made me understand why most women would gladly hack their husbands into bits if only it were legal under such circumstances. "Ladies and gentlemen of the jury, my client simply could not take another moment of being ignored." I said to Adam, "And furthermore, why don't you go fuck yourself, you disgusting weasel?"

I went to my computer, turned it on, and cleaned out my email inbox. He could dump me after losing his father, just like he and his mother and his crispy sisters had sent Bill off to face his demise alone. But if I had anything to say about it, I would choose my own end.

·13·

NURSES CAN TAKE THE PRESSURE

Obviously, I Don't Have a Penis

For my third treatment in this second set of six, Regina numbed me up. I chided her. "It'll all be fine, after my sexual reassignment surgery."

She pulled her head back. Her eyes widened. She was overdoing her surprise reaction but remained sincerely curious. She had to be careful in this modern world of genital fluidity and political correctness.

"I was just kidding."

Regina chuckled. Pal.

Dr. Hellman entered swiftly. He looked into my eyes. He knew I needed contact. He was very red-faced. I asked, "Have you been out in the sun?'

"That, and I was rushing down here."

He must have been sensitive about his red face. He was panting some.

"I'll come back later to talk about the plaque, after your injections."

He left as quickly as he had entered. He never returned.

Being neurotically inclined, or perhaps overly sensitive, I thought I had gotten too personal about the condition of his face and had repelled him into disappearance. I do not know if I like this power I think I have. Dr. Scavone, the quiet one, came in to do the treatment, with Regina as his assistant. He Swiss cheese needled me only down the right side. (The last time, did they mostly go down the left side? Dammit! I don't think so!) I was still so concerned with this lopsided treatment. I was still bent upward. Still constricted with a ring in the middle. My paranoia kicked in, as usual, and I wondered if all they were doing was collecting money from the insurance company for these possibly bogus treatments. Were they really getting at it as strongly as they needed to? In the big picture, it felt like they were poking holes in something that really needed to be sliced.

After Dr. Scavone was finished I asked him about the bent dorsal side of my penis, the top, with a concerned quaver in my voice, as non-accusatory as possible, "Did you miss the saddle area?"

Dr. Scavone ripened into an irritated and defensive ogre. "It's not like painting. I don't paint the whole thing." Then he softened, apologetically, "You know it better. You live with it."

He did not instill confidence.

I then said, attempting to cover my bossy inquiry, "I'm not trying to tell you how to do your job, it's just, I like to know. It's interesting."

He said, "I didn't take it like that." He was lying. Or embarrassed about his outcry. Or simply distant from understanding himself, like so many men with penises.

Perhaps I talked to him too much like I would a hairdresser—A little off the top. I often provoke discomfort in reserved people. I am observant and verbal, but usually kind. Dr. Scavone stood there for a while looking at me, quietly annoyed, waiting to hear if I had any other irritating queries, then cleaned up and left. When a professional or anyone I know gets exceptionally quiet I imagine it's because they are in a high state of discomfort. —Goodbye Dr. Scavone. Go struggle with yourself somewhere else. And I'll do the same. We all suffer.

When I was getting ready to leave, Regina, now my friend,

remained. I told her, apologetically, "I feel kind of stupid for my dare-I-ask-the-cranky-doctor behavior, but that was kind of a weird experience, right?"

By the subtle nod in her eyes, she agreed. She did not risk any great behavioral agreement and could deny her affirmation if pushed. Smart primate.

I continued, self-soothing and people-pleasing all at once, "But I will be okay since this is not life-threatening. But it does have psychological effects."

Regina said, "Obviously, I don't have a penis, but I'm sure it does."

I said, attempting connection, "Many women get double mastectomies—which must be real hard."

"Yeah," she said.

Regina was silent and humble in the face of life's nastiness. I wanted to reach across and touch her. Or better, I would have liked her to just put a hand on my arm and say, "It's so hard being human. But we're in this together, matey. I love you so much."

Regina did not do that. She had already quietly ganged up on Dr. Scavone with me and that was enough love for one visit. I left, feeling low and bullied by Dr. Scavone and cynical about this treatment. Were they just waving a dead cat over my head and then trying to get me to believe that Jesus had just walked on my back? My mood was in a dumpster. I felt rejected by Adam. My base was coming undone.

I took my path home through the park. The entrance was at 69th Street—cruel number. A beautiful thin man in his twenties in a striped brown-and-yellow terrycloth tank top with a perfectly coiffed short beard and sunglasses, speaking Italian or something that may as well have been, was walking in front of me. He was so attractive, and I was feeling very much like an aged gay Humbert Humbert from *Lolita*, but sort of fat, with my penis wrapped in self-sticking, tight surgical gauze. Deeper into the park, I felt my old abandonment fear rising up and started to think about how my life had been filled with painful disappointment. Not that

I have had more disappointments than others, though maybe I have. It is just that each disappointment feels like abandonment, like I am going to die alone, reviled, basically for being who I am. This outlook is pathetically disordered, as I am truly loved on earth. *What a Poor Boy*, the backup singers would sarcastically sing at me in Nick Drake's song. I replay it all the time.

When I was one month old my mother became pregnant. She was naturally horrified, being a woman who was having children way too young, more out of lower socioeconomic strata habit than anything else. In addition to my sister, who was two and a half, and the newly hatched me, my Momma had nine months ahead of her of a complete repeat of what she had just been through. The lore is that I was an exceptionally docile child that needed almost no care, except that I ate nonstop, especially bananas. In fact, I was mostly left alone, taking forever to develop. I imagine myself in my playpen, my pregnant mother twenty-two years old, occasionally walking by and tossing a piece of fruit in my cage for sustenance.

After Charlie was born, I still was not developing properly. I did nothing but lie around and eat. I never hit any of the normal markers. My mother, with the agreement of the pediatrician, Dr. John Charles, decided that it was time to test me for what they called retardation. My mother sobbed on the phone to her mother. Next thing you know, Nanny, two doors away in her little white cottage, about half the size of our little yellow house, whisked me off to her boot camp. That was Friday. By Monday, I was rolling, creeping, sitting up and even gurgling. When I was returned to my mother, she asked, "What did you do?"

My grandmother, Neapolitan by way of Newark, a childcare expert and someone who saved over fifty thousand dollars by watching other people's kids said, "There's nothing wrong with him. He's just lazy. I told him to sit up. He understood me. And when he didn't, I whacked him. When I told him to roll over and he didn't do that either, I whacked him again."

My mother was grateful. I was soon being whacked into

crawling and other physical activity. I never said any words until one day, at about three years old, I spoke in complete sentences. The developmental rigors of each person are unique.

I do not know if I ever bonded completely with my mother as a baby. I was very close to my grandmother. I do remember being very close to my mother in elementary school. She often saved me from the neighborhood bullies. We both were very sensitive to our surroundings—décor, people, the air. I have never been through any regression therapy to get to the bottom of my severe problem with abandonment. I have logged in monstrous hours talking about it with therapists. Most of my living days I haven't quite felt completely at home anywhere. Oddly, at the same time, I can feel at home anywhere, in a dissociated corporate hotel room kind of way. Or like a dog who has had four owners and bonds to anyone readily.

With this Peyronie's disease and my partner of eighteen years wanting to leave, I felt alone and vulnerable, distant to everything around me, fully rejected, just the not-at-home-anywhere feeling taking the entire stage. This was in alignment with how I really was in the world and had been since my beginning. It made sense. There is an upside to being cut off emotionally at the quick. You get to really notice things around you from a great distance. The cold visual cortex takes charge. Colors and shapes are clear. Life is a distant movie. Images get brighter.

As I continued to walk across the park, New Yorkers were enjoying their special clans. New York City is not a melting pot, really, but a patchwork of self-sorting groups, each one vying for supremacy. Some negative voice grabbed at me—It's like late nineteenth-century European nationalism and the horrors of all that.

Then my fix-it voice took over—The only thing that connects us is our basic human nature. All the various traits of different racial and cultural groups are good because diversity, when propagated, makes for a sturdy species. We should interbreed as quickly as possible. The Internet, though helpful, has not done what I think is its job: to erase all borderlines. No one is better than anyone else. All these fucking groups, with their need to feel superior, should disband and mingle. Immediately.

Clearly I was feeling left out, a strange cripple among a healthy humanity that was too busy to include me. Diatribe. Diatribe.

Adam was at work, making two-thirds of our money in a tower on Broadway and 50th Street. Did he never really love his father? Seemed so. Maybe. Very little. I thought again about Lars von Trier's *Breaking the Waves*, a movie I could never entirely sit through, and it made complete sense that Adam should just go ahead and have sex with other people, not only in a Don't-Ask-Don't-Tell arrangement, but however the hell he wanted to. I would be happy to watch. This could maybe relieve some pressure. He did not have to leave me.

Soon after the third treatment, I sat him down at the white Formica table with the blond wood trim in our "Large Open Studio." We had bought the table at the antique store Studio 111, in Palm Springs, a few years prior, for our little apartment in Queens, and shipped it east. I thought the table was 1980s hideous, but Adam made a big push for it as a perfectly sized four-seater that could fold down into a two-seater and even be folded down on both sides to be stored in the back of a closet. He was right about its utility so we bought it. I did not get as excited about this purchase as I did about the sweet little Danish modern nightstand, the top made from that lovely orange wood, held up by four thin legs, each one made of two black coated metal rods, one rod straight up and one angled inward. There was also a slatted shelf below, for magazines, made from the same metal rods, only a half centimeter in diameter. It was something I had never seen before, and I still have it and love it, even though the drawer can fall apart in the front right corner, the tongue and groove not always holding together.

Sometimes, grabbing onto furniture can save you. We all have strong relationships with inanimate objects as children. Rilke said something like, "Avoid people. Have relationships with objects. They won't disappoint you."

—Damn right, you isolated Bohemian!

Like many long-term couples, our sex life had been partially replaced by shopping, and as a gay couple, we fit the stereotype of being fussy decorators who had long discussions about size, color, material and vibe. That evening, sitting at the low-vibe but useful table that Adam had chosen, the folding ugly beast from Palm Springs, and letting my anger fly, my numbed penis having regained its feeling, I tried to set Adam straight. "You were unemployed for years and you put me through hell. You were a disaster. Your anxiety attacks had anxiety attacks. You had fucking face cancer and I stayed with you through thick and thin. Remember how you cried almost every day because they took your beautiful little blond face and ripped it open and you felt so vulnerable and awful?"

"Yeah."

Adam endured a horrible Mohs surgery the last year we lived in Los Angeles. The basal cell carcinoma on the left side of his nose was much deeper than they had expected. When you go in for this procedure, they cannot tell you how long it is going to take. They numb your face and they take out the cancer. Then they take the piece they took out and look for clear margins under a microscope. If there is no cancer on any edge they do not need to cut any more. Adam had to be cut three times deep.

The surgeon made a hole in the side of Adam's nose the size of a dime. In order to take care of this hole on a patient, they scalpel a Z-shaped cut starting on the forehead. The larger the hole to fill, the higher up the forehead they must begin the cut because more skin is needed. After they make the Z cut, which goes right down the middle of the nose and across the cheek, the cheek skin is pulled over the hole and then the entire Z is stitched. It's a monster movie. After that mess heals, you go back for many visits, getting your face scrubbed with sandpaper to smooth it all out. Adam had all this done to him the same year all three of our pets died—two cats and a dog—and his television writing career ended. It was not long after that that we decamped for Queens.

"Moreover! You selfish asshole, you were raised by monsters. Your parents had nothing to do with each other and I have spent most of my adult life trying to turn you into someone who cares about being intimate. I almost succeeded. And you think you are going to leave me? Right now? What the fuck is wrong with you? You are going to get even more diseases as you get older. We both are. You are going to continue to have problems. And me, too! This is how it is!"

He sat there without any expression, like a trout on ice.

"Your father's death did something to you. Sure, I get it. But even worse things are going to happen. That's how life is, you miserable pussy. I'm furious."

Adam reached across the ugly table, like he always did, because he hated when I became angry.

"Okay. Okay. It's okay. Why are you yelling?"

"You either stay committed to me, fully, forever, or I am out of here, I mean it."

I meant it.

He dug in even deeper. He gave me the silent face. He considered what I was saying. His wheels turned. His face showed no sign of change. Adam always hated to lose.

·14·

THE THINKING MAN'S PENIS

For a Better Society

When I am alone, I like to think. When things are very stressful, I like to think hard. When things are very stressful and my penis has been through a lot and my man wants to leave me, I can't stop thinking for a second.

I like an orderly life. I do not enjoy chaos. I prefer stability and repeated evenings of dinner with best friends. I like my man to be my man. It is a solid feeling. I thrive on intimacy that does not expire. For me, a long-term relationship makes a lot of sense. Adam is similar for dissimilar reasons. He needs continuity more as a backdrop; I need it as the foreground. He likes me to be around while the television is on. I like the television off so we can talk. Every relationship is its own torture rack. When we met, Adam and I were both on the rise. We were young, educated, creative, male, white, attractive and energized, with a growing network of busy careerists and fun folks. Cultural biases were in our favor. I never promised Adam I would become wealthy, but I did present outsized ambition that showed signs of a monster payout when we first met. Turns out, I simply picked careers that were easy to fail in. Movie star. Playwright. Why not try for nuclear fusion in a coke bottle?

Adam wanted money.

I wanted fame.

Adam wanted to travel.

I did, too, but I wanted sex more.

We were not exactly meant for each other. I was more combative. He was more stubborn. I was more affectionate, but a little diffuse in my attention. He was cooler, but mathematically, more sexually loyal. I was a bigger risk-taker. Adam craved normalcy. I hated to work in an office. Adam thrived in structured groups. I am basically Irish and Italian, from a long-ago, working class, farmy bunch. Adam is basically a second boater (the one that arrived after the Mayflower), architectural and commercial. Optimistic couples therapists would often tell us we were great compliments to each other, but they were in the save-the-relationship business. As so many people who are in the middle of breakups have sighed, "A relationship really shouldn't have to be so difficult."

I would love to say I am a total alcoholic or a survivor of immense abuse or something else very clear that has a strong and well-worn path to recovery. But I merely struggle in the middle of the pack, like most people, occasionally getting drunk and stoned but mostly sober, occasionally being victimized, occasionally the victimizer, loved, unloved, sometimes powerful, often invisible, a mixed bag. My mother hit me when angry, but not every day. My sister was handsy, but so was I. My mother raged, but only when manic, not when she was depressed. My father drank, but many years he did not, though one year he did have a love affair with whiskey that almost drove my mother out the door. This was during the era after Charlie was mowed down by the car, so leaving would have been exceptionally inconvenient. My parents were a team. They loved me, not exactly for who I was, but for what I was, their son. They were always very romantic with each other, dancing in the kitchen after dinner. Sometimes a fight would break out in the car over a disagreement about reality and my mother would yell, "Pull over!" and she would jump out and walk toward home for a while, until my father pulled up alongside her and coaxed her back in. They were young and lively.

I had years when I had no friends at all and years when I was very popular. I was always attractive to some people, attracted to others. Some have found me to be disgusting and repellant. I have always been the moody creative, anxiety and depression wanting to grab at my skull. Because I am basically sane, I have fought hard to find my middle, my calm. I have mostly succeeded. I have almost never had to pay an overdue bill. I have pushed hard to be alive and spontaneous on the highway of life while always making sure my rational mind drives the bus. I have strived to be clear-headed, compassionate and easygoing.

I punched Adam in the face. This was six years before my penis started to bend. We were visiting San Francisco from Los Angeles at the tail end of a long period when I was hardly drinking, not by any personal decree, but because I was busy and had more interest in working than in hanging out in the backyard chugging down cheap merlot. One of our best friends, Hogan, one of the guys I had met the same night I first met Adam, had moved up to the Bay Area for his position as the Grand Poobah in the human resources department of a placement firm that focused on artistic directors and designers. He lived in Potrero Hill with that great view north to Downtown. The Transamerica Tower, the Bay Bridge. Romantic. Vertiginous. Our other friend, Susan, who threw the dinner party where I met Adam and Hogan, joined us from Los Angeles. Hogan, Susan and Adam were all committed to a solid Friday night booze fest. I was dreading the weekend. I went along to get along. It felt like a college party weekend about to erupt, and we were all long out of college.

After everyone arrived at Hogan's house, including Hogan, who had worked a little later than he had wanted to, we made plans for the evening. Hogan's roommate, Grieg, joined Susan, Hogan, Adam and me for the Friday night revelry. Hogan's rental house was huge. There were more roommates, but they were away for the weekend. The fun building was perched on stilts on the side of the hill that is Potrero and had back decks overlooking other houses that were similarly clad in clapboard. Hogan's siding was periwinkle blue.

We ate a huge Vietnamese dinner a few blocks away. Grieg, lanky, younger than we were, perfectly attractive in the pale skin, light eyes, black hair kind of way, brother to Hogan's boss, and all-around charmer, was easy to watch all night because he was lanky, young, attractive and charming. Adam and I both competed for his attention. Once I realized what we were doing, I pulled back some, for aesthetic reasons and to protect myself from braying like a middle-aged Elizabeth Taylor in an Edward Albee play. Additionally, though I was not in Grieg's league, I was still competitive and decided Grieg had received enough of my energy. This attractive man got Adam excited. Understandably. I was excited, too, but since I knew the guy was both straight and not an experimenter, what was the use in even caring?

After dinner, Hogan decided it was time to go to the bar where they served scorpion bowls. Ever been to college? These are the wretched booze bowls made from gin, vodka, rum and fruit juices, all mixed together to get you and your pals maximally shitfaced as quickly as possible. Resistance to swallowing all that sugar? Why not add fuel to the fire?

We were sucking down this noxious brew, straws in the brightly multicolored tureens, livers charged, ready for anything. We got drunk in twenty-six minutes. The bowls were expensive so we decided to decamp to the local Irish shithole for beer. When we got there, I could not imagine drinking anything more. My metabolism was lightning fast in those days and I could go from drink to drunk to hangover in forty minutes. My head was pounding.

So water was important.

As Adam and the others sucked down their beers, I decided to fix my head and get a big glass of water from the bar. No ice. The bar was deep-brown with a waxy buildup, the bartender tall and sandy.

"Can I have a glass of water, please? No ice."

"Sure."

He poured. I returned to the table. I swigged a mouthful.

Adam asked me, "Can I have a sip?"

"Why don't you get your own? My head is pounding."

"I just want a sip."

"Okay, but just a sip. I mean it."

I handed the glass to the snockered Adam. His eyes were distant and mischievous. His small defiant child, the little beast that craves power more than anything else, took over, and I could tell I was in for a sour treat.

Adam drank the whole glass of water, slammed down the glass and laughed.

I remained calm.

"Okay, very funny. Now go get me a glass of water."

"No."

"Get me a glass of water."

"No."

Something about being alcohol-infused. Something about his childhood. Something about wanting to impress his friends. Something deep about the joy of humiliating another, the closest one in. I could not believe that I chose to live with this man. He really liked to make me the object of ridicule whenever he was drinking.

"Get me a glass of water, Adam. My head is pounding. You know it. Get it."

"Get your own water."

"Get it."

"No."

"Get it, you asshole."

Susan, small and capable, who had had enough, got up and said, "Oh for Christ's sake, I'll get you a glass of water."

Susan went to the brown, waxy bar, got a glass and brought it to me.

Adam glowed with the thrill of not having to cave in. I thought for a second that I should just swallow the experience, but I knew what was coming and I was not able to stop myself.

I threw the glass of water in Adam's face. This, of course, broke up the party. Adam stood up fast. The nerve of me! Grieg left the table and headed home. So did I, finished for the night. Booze. Booze. Booze.

Back at the large rental house, Grieg went to his bedroom, getting ready to go someplace else with younger, better-looking people. I was alone in the kitchen, drank a few glasses of water and started to think about what would happen next. Would it just end and would Adam finally understand that I was not going to endure public humiliation ever again? Maybe we could all pop in a movie. Anything.

No such luck. The front door slammed open. Adam, Susan and Hogan entered. Adam was on a furious tear. He went right into the kitchen to get a large glass of water, clearly with the intention of getting back at me. This, I decided, was not going to happen. I had rarely ever hit a person, but sometimes you have to strike. I had a sister who would hit me or pull my hair because, well, it was fun for her. Early one evening, when I was twelve, it was my turn to put the frozen french fries in the oven before my mother got back from work. I was in my room playing my guitar. My sister insisted I get up to do it immediately. I insisted that as soon as I was done practicing my guitar I would go do it. She told me to march into the kitchen. I said no. She grabbed a snatch of my hair and said, "Go now."

I said, "Let go of my hair."

"Not until you wipe that look off your face."

I did have a look on my face. It was superior.

"Let go of my hair, now."

"Not until you get that look off your face."

I dropped the judgmental look. She let go. I stood up. I punched her so hard she fell to the ground. She never touched me again. This memory, a good smash that turned out to be a smash, goaded me into action that rotten night on Potrero Hill. It had worked before.

There Adam was, with the glass of water in his hand. Years of tension between us reached the breaking point. No longer would I simply be myself at parties only to have a drunk Adam say something awful about me in front of everyone. No longer the nasty little practical jokes that telegraphed to the world that I was but a mousey plaything. I simply grabbed the offending arm.

"Adam, put the glass down. It's over."

"No."

"It's over. I won. Put the glass down."

"No."

"Adam, if you try to throw that glass of water on me, I'm going to hit you."

"I'm just getting back at you."

"No. You lost. It's over. Put the glass down."

"I'm getting back at you."

"I'm going to hit you."

He did not believe me. He would not relent. While still holding his arm that held the water-filled glass with my left hand, I took my right hand off his other arm and punched him on his left cheekbone, hard enough so he would feel it but not hard enough to break anything. I was not a maniac. I was exacting. He held his ground.

Then I jerked his glass-holding arm so hard that the glass flew out of his hand and smashed into pieces all over the terra cotta tile of the kitchen. Grieg heard this and flew out the front door. His parents were alcoholics, so, you know, enough already. Susan and Hogan were powerless, both smaller than both of us. Then, for good measure, I hit Adam again, a little lower, with an open hand, so it was more of a Now-Get-The-Fuck-Away-From-Me slap.

"I can't believe you did this to me. I can't believe you."

"Don't you ever fucking humiliate me again in front of anyone. Ever."

Adam ran out the front door, sat at a bus stop for a bus that never arrived, jumped in a random cab, went to the airport and flew home. I had to endure the next day being with our friends, who were Adam's friends first. They looked at me like I was a mafia hitman.

The next morning, Susan and Hogan went to visit a mutual friend. It was clear I was not welcome. I walked around San Francisco alone. I ate a turkey-with-melted-cheese sandwich on Larkin or Hyde, above Lombard Street, at a small, struggling café. It was beautiful outside and I thought it would just make a lot of sense to find an apartment nearby and just eat, alone, at that café for the rest of my life. I felt like an enormous bully. A pariah. A vulgar, not clever, slob.

Story goes: Adam went home and decided that we were through. He made a list of what to divide. I drove back to Los Angeles, quiet in the car with Susan, Adam's best friend, the kind of best friend to a gay man that believes her gay is the greatest and cutest gay who ever lived. I made a small case for what happened the night before and saw quickly that I held no truck, so we turned to small talk for over three hundred miles down I-5, passed Cowschwitz, the enormous stockyards that stink of shit and pain, and arrived home by dinner. She dropped me off at my house in Hollywood, quickly, and hauled off out of there to the safety of her apartment at the beach.

Adam was silent. I was calm. I put away my clothes and things. I apologized for hitting him. He cried. I apologized again. He said, "You can't ever hit me. If you ever hit me again—"

"I won't. I've never hit you before. I'm not a hitter. I'm sorry. I'm really sorry. I feel awful. I could have done a million other things. I never should have hit you. I should not have stayed at the bar. I should have just gone home after the scorpion bowls. The booze and the sugar. It was an awful night and I'm a monster."

I felt guilty that I had punched him, but I was happy that I had put a huge dent in his ability to joyfully make fun of me or tease me in public. We stayed together. The mortgage continued to be paid and the sex was passable. But nothing ever ends that neatly. Especially with people.

Two years later, we were walking up Highland in Los Angeles to sign up to attend Joni Mitchell's Green Flag Song exhibition at the

Lev Moross gallery. We were talking and we missed the entrance. If you live in Los Angeles you may appreciate the common mistake that many of us make. It is hard to remember if something is on Highland or on La Brea. This is similar to the problem of Vermont and Hillhurst in Los Feliz, near Griffith Park. Parallel commercial streets, separated by only a few blocks—you sometimes forget where that particular bookstore is, or that art gallery, or for that matter, where the hell you parked your car.

I remembered the gallery to be on Highland, but we did miss it because we were yacking, and Adam asked, "Where is it? You never know where you are. You always make this mistake."

"I know it's on Highland. I know it is. We must have missed it. But maybe, maybe it's on La Brea. Let me check my phone."

Service was spotty. Adam continued to yell at me. "Always! Always!"

"Okay, okay. I know it's frustrating. We'll find it. Calm down."

I am not sure where Adam had to be. I did not know why he was so upset. It became very clear to me on that day that time was the most important thing for him. Not that he was afraid to waste time but that he was furious about any time that went unmanaged. I am, ridiculously, nothing like that—I stay up until all hours, like to see projects through no matter where the sun is sitting. I always knew he liked to have a grip on every minute of the day, but he had grown much more vigilant about his clock problem. Later, he explained to me that as a kid he was so bullied that planning his walks home at particular times is what his entire elementary school years were all about. Just awful. But one could, once knowing the root cause, let this loosen up a bit?

I continued to check my phone and Adam continued to yell at me.

"You always do this. You always do."

"Okay, okay, enough. I know. You're right. Highland and La Brea, I never know. They confuse me. Stop yelling. I'll find it. I'm sorry."

The phone kicked in. I got the address. The gallery was on Highland. We had missed it because we were talking. The seven hundred block. We went back, signed up, got tickets and left.

Adam continued. "You don't care about the time. You always make this mistake. Always."

This, of course, is not true at all.

"Honey, we were talking and we missed it. It all worked out. No one ever does anything always. You know it."

Something had already gone off in his head. Whatever the synaptic conversion, it was not letting loose. Perhaps, in addition to his time concerns, it had something to do with feeling like he never got his way? Or perhaps his frustration about his television writing career had become so severe, his latest showrunner boss—notoriously uninterested in his talent—destroying his self-esteem so entirely that he had to take it all out on someone? Or maybe it was simply an understandable hatred for having to walk up busy Highland Avenue in the broiling sun in the newly dubbed "Melrose Media District?" He continued to yell.

"It's like you don't ever think of me. You just do whatever you want and you never think about what I have to do."

"That's not true. I'm going to go home now. We are finished. Please stop yelling."

"No, I won't. You always do this. Always."

"Get the fuck away from me, then. It was an honest mistake."

"No."

"Get away. We got the tickets. We just missed the place. That's all. It's no big deal."

"No. You always do this. You always do it."

"Stop telling me what I always do. I'm going home. I don't want to be around you another minute. Get the fuck away from me."

"No. I won't."

"Get the fuck away from me."

"No!" he yelled into my face. He had to have satisfaction. He would not let me pass.

I kicked him in the shin and went home.

That was the last time I struck him.

I felt terrible that I had kicked him, having come from a family of hitters and kickers and hair pullers. On a boring winter afternoon, I'd run around the dining room table with my siblings, all of us brandishing huge kitchen knives, pretending we were going to stab each other, and had hit my sister in the head with a bird house and my brother in the head with a metal shoe stretcher—I knew how destructive that all was. I apologized to Adam on the spot, then I apologized for two weeks. I felt awful. This was the second time I had hit him in two years. I was so angry with Adam and I lashed out physically and I knew this to be very wrong. Adam accepted my apology.

I attended the Joni Mitchell art opening with Hogan and a few other friends. Adam had to work and was not available. While talking to a small crowd of us, Joni said about war, "It would be better if men just went out into a field with bows and arrows."

I added, "Or into an arena to play war games."

She liked that idea and held my gaze for a moment. This appeared to be my moment to connect with her on a deeper level. I tried, but trying to be too interesting I said something off-topic and Joni lost interest in me and moved on to other admirers. Later, she signed my *Turbulent Indigo* CD. I told her I listened to her music almost daily. She seemed a bit creeped out by that. We did not become best friends. When I returned from the event, Adam was already home from work. He asked me about Joni. Then we talked.

We agreed it was time to go back to couples counseling. We had been before, twice, both times working in very cognitive ways, being taught to never say never and to always avoid always, to be more loving toward each other, to express positive gratitude for even the smallest generosities—the kinds of things you can read about by searching for any book that sounds like *A Couple's Handbook to Bliss* or *Twelve Easy Steps to Love and Respect* or *The Secret to Love is Giving Some*. This time, we made an appointment at the Gay and Lesbian Center up on Schrader, in Hollywood. It was inexpensive and convenient. We went for our intake as a couple. The usual questions were asked.

When the intake man, a mild-mannered homosexual with

strong humanist tendencies and a small bald spot in dark ginger hair, asked us, well into the interview, "Have either of you ever struck or hit the other person?" Adam and I both laughed. There was the punch in the face in San Francisco a couple of years earlier, the recent kick in the shin because we got lost looking for the gallery for Joni's art show, and the time many years ago when we had spit at each other because I put on the sausages for my birthday party and Adam had had a different plan for their timing and it turned into a ridiculous fight. I thought I was doing him a favor getting the sausages going on the barbecue, saving him some effort. He thought I was being very controlling, putting the sausages on before he wanted them on. It was venomous. We behaved like cobras.

Neither Adam nor I thought of the other as abusive. These three physical encounters had taken place over a fifteen-year span. One could easily call them unusual events. The therapist explained, "We are going to have to set up appointments to interview you separately."

"Really?" I asked.

"Yes. Whenever there is a possibility of domestic abuse, the protocol is to make appointments to interview each of you privately."

"Huh."

Our laughter died down. But we still did not believe we were in an abusive relationship. All we wanted was some subsidized gay couples counseling, but we all must jump through hoops when asking for cheap things. We set up the appointments back to back.

A week later we returned. A different therapist, one who was a specialist in assessing domestic abuse, bearded and calm, a lithe man in somber dark-brown tweed, met with Adam and interviewed him first. After he left, I went in. I prepared myself to be declared the abuser since, besides the equal spitting in each other's faces over the birthday sausages, the score was very uneven, as I had both punched Adam in San Francisco and kicked him on Highland in Los Angeles. I answered all the questions honestly.

"Have you ever hit your partner?"

"Yes, there were three incidents."

I explained the three incidents. The spitting. The SFO punch. The Joni Kick.

"I'm sorry I did those things."

"Why do you think you did them?"

"Well, Adam has a way of publicly humiliating me is really the biggest one. He likes to make sure I am put in my place."

"When does this happen?"

"If we're at a party, and especially when it is his closest friends who hold him in great esteem, I can do almost nothing ... something as simple as dance too much or talk too much and I am attacked verbally. Made fun of. Given withering looks. Sometimes it's a huge practical joke at my expense."

"Does this make you angry?"

"Like I want to kill."

"What do you do about it?"

"For years, nothing. Then for a few months I would insist that I take my own car so if things got really nasty I could leave."

"Did that work?"

"It did. Then I stopped taking my own car and it started to happen again."

"Then what did you do?"

"Well, you know I punched him in the face in San Francisco."

"Are there ever any substances involved?"

"We were both drinking. Yes. But when I hit him, I was pretty much clear-headed. When I kicked him on Highland, we were stone-cold sober and no one else was around, really. I just had to get him away from me. He wouldn't stop yelling at me."

The questions continued. I felt heard and not too ashamed. I tried to wrap it up in Adam's favor. I had been through a lot of therapy over the years.

"I think it's this. I had a very verbal mother who ruled the roost. I do the same at home. I think Adam feels overwhelmed and powerless in our house so when we go out he uses the energy of his friends for backup to knock me down. I kind of understand it."

"Uh-huh."

"He is afraid of my anger. He really hates it when I get angry. Like the world is going to end. His parents never fought. Mine did. He gets super upset when I get mad at him and express it. He tells me I should never talk to him with any anger ever."

"Do you think that's possible?"

"Maybe. I don't know. I can be overbearing. Maybe I am too critical and he's afraid of me."

"Maybe. We will call you in two days with results after your case is presented."

"Great. Thanks."

I left. Two days later we did get the call. The outcome was that Adam was the abuser and I only hit him to protect myself. I was surprised. I felt relieved but sad. I thought we would at least be implicated equally. But no. Adam, the lighter, thinner, blonder, blue-eyed, sweeter one harbored more devil soul than this darker he-bag.

The recommendation was for Adam to go to a group session of abusers to learn to work on his anger. There is something called the cycle of abuse, where the abuser starts out fine, gains your confidence, and then, once you are in, attacks. The attack is horrific and usually works not only to inflict aggression but to damage the self-esteem of the victim. Then the abuser feels guilty and apologizes, often with entreaties for forgiveness, maybe even with a special meal or a gift involved, and if the partner is receptive, they get close again, only to repeat the cycle. This sounded just about right. There were even handouts with diagrams that looked like they could have been drawn in our living room. Of course, the behavior was not nonstop. The problem with most systems and diagrams is they assume endlessness. Ours was intermittent, certainly.

Adam was a dutiful student and made it through the twelve-week course. Many of the attendees were court ordered to be there. The treatment was a bit over-the-top, but it worked. If nothing else, being forced to see that a cycle of abuse can even exist opened his eyes. His father was abusive. His mother had a sharp mouth. He learned it somewhere. He just had to become aware of it and dismantle the pattern.

Adam asked me to never tell anyone about this. But it has been many years since I kicked Adam in the shin over the Joni tickets and he attended "abuse camp," where he learned a thing or two and so stopped with the public humiliation. Adam even publicly read a story about it with humor and grace. I believe that his transformation can be taken for what it was: a triumph. In the end, it was a testament to his ability to change, and though embarrassing, it was not the whole of him, just the drinking-with-friends of him or fear of out-of-control time of him, mixed with unconscious inertia.

You watch all these plays and movies and television specials where the abused woman finally walks out of the marriage. It's all about empowerment. You rarely hear a story where the abuser gets better and then the relationship gets better. You do hear stories about addicts who recover and then see their marriages improve. In our case, after the Joni kick, there were no more displays of physical aggression from my end. Adam cut back on the public humiliation. A few times he would rib me a little bit at some book club or some birthday shebang and I would loudly stop it in front of everyone with a brusque, simple statement like, "You just said that I look fat in this shirt in front of everyone and it seems to me that it was said with the intention to inflict pain."

Once he learned that I would always speak up, even if we were in front of the Queen of England, that the cycle of abuse would never be able to accelerate, that he really did have a desire to inflict damage and I was always going to announce it when it reared its head, he was able to tap into what he learned at abuse camp and stop his endless garbage. He became hyperaware of his own impulses and of my inner life. He softened. He simply softened. I grew less vigilant.

But still (still thinking) isn't withholding love while I am going through my penis treatments a form of abuse? Isn't the threat of a breakup, unless I do what he tells me, a form of abuse? Like I should go to work for Wells Fargo or something and then he would be happy with me? But then, don't people break up over money all the time? Yes they do. If we have to break up because I am not an income dynamo, well, there is nothing I can do to make Adam cease his resentment of me, so perhaps we would be better off if we ended this difficult partnership. I can take my half and go. I am immediately employable as a few boring things.

Our relationship was never easy. We came to love each other very slowly. It did not even look like love. It looked harsh. The first ten years, our love was inconsistently supportive, often competitive, and at times, nonexistent, with only cool anger making our worlds go round. Our straight rock-climber friend, Russell, always said, "You two are perfect for each other. Who else would have you?" He based his opinion mostly on our ability to quip in funny ways, and our shared lack of sentimentality and nonexistent sacred cows. This did not mean, though, that we were perfect for each other. We just found common ground, and the common ground was rough. Not unlike an arranged marriage in a traditional culture since our meeting was arranged by our college friends, it was figured out by others that we would be good together since we were gay, unattached and the same age. Plus, everyone had been to college in Boston in the '80s and we all had the same reference points so it was easy. Then, like with anything that is arranged, we had to face what was really there. Certain nights, feeling terrified and alone, I would fantasize about leaving.

But where would I go? Back to mother? Move into a cheap bachelor apartment in Mar Vista off Venice Boulevard, a big brown fridge in the one and only room, like the one I lived in after I moved out of old Lillian's guest house in Brentwood because she was so homophobic? Or even better, find a large man with uneven features who would put up with my uneven income because he was so proud to have formerly-pretty, once lovely-penised me? I would have to bring a lot of old snapshots.

Couples fall apart. I could maybe let this whole partnership go, but like the example of my mother and father—one so loquacious on the phone you better prepare your ears, while the other one, after a short conversation, just wants to get to the point about the latest weather patterns—I have seen relationships that should not have endured last a long time. People do stay. But when a person is not appreciated and it feels ongoing and one's penis is actually getting better, not worse, the option to take off is enticing.

I looked at our light-gray Ikea shoeboxes of photos. Did I really want to have to make copies of everything?

Sure, I could do that. I have a scanner.

CDs and books were no longer a problem in a breakup—Please, take them! Take them all! I have everything in digital! Moldy old paperbacks make me sneeze!

Furniture is site-specific so whoever wants whatever for their new place, have it.

Friends? What about friends? Well, those who love you will stick around. Those that do not will disappear. What a great way to force those hands!

And the memories? They will remain with or without the person. Anyway, couldn't I just chuck the memories into a big red bag, haul them over my shoulder like Santa Claus, and give them to myself as presents whenever I needed a little Christmas? The longer I could stay with Adam the more important those memories would become, but are the memories worth the staying? Isn't that just a bunch of sentimental malarkey?

I had been pondering only the negatives. Like my childhood, which was both horrendous and joyful, my adult life with Adam had been comprised of more than just the colossal drags of anger, disrespect and coldness. In order to take the inventory of this relationship, I would have to consider the good times, too, which, truly, took up more hours than our troubled minutes. Now was the time. It came fast and thick. I got to thinking in the other direction.

Like the first really good date, when he made me the clam sauce and we had sex on his dark purple and blue paisley patterned futon and even though it was awkward it was exciting and we sort of fit. I was very attracted to him, the sweetie, the heart wanting what it wanted.

Like how he got me my first auditions on the television shows where he worked, eventually helping me land an ongoing gig as the snarky gay waiter on *Dharma & Greg*, and how I then realized I was probably never going to be anything more than a snarky gay waiter on any television show and lost my Hollywood morale, so he encouraged me to figure out what I should do next.

Like the trip to Northern California where I bought the touristy clay maroon Agate Cove Inn mug with the white foamy edging from Mendocino that sat next to me every day while I worked at the computer, that is still sitting next to me right now. The incredible oxygen-rush we experienced in the Redwood forest on that same trip. We really always traveled well together.

The ten-year anniversary trip to France. Well, we fought a lot in France. Mostly about driving, maps, the usual couple stuff in a manual transmission rental car in a foreign country. I slammed the door and jumped out of the car high on a bluff overlooking Cassis. Kind of like my mother, but with manual transmission on a windswept lump of mountain overlooking the Mediterranean. Fuck it. Fuck him. Fuck France. *Va te faire enculer*! But otherwise, we always loved to go to France. That was positive.

That crazy day when we were house shopping in Los Angeles, about five years into our relationship. I woke up one morning at 6:00, very unusual for me, with what I thought were gas pains. I got through that. Then, by noon, while we were looking at a hideous house on Waring Avenue on a half lot with a garage-turned-family-room and an overall spastic layout, I said, emphatically, "Let's buy this! It's great!" The realtor got excited. Adam thought I was nuts. We jumped back into his red Cabriolet convertible and within thirty seconds I said, "Take me to the hospital." I knew I was dying, but not of what. He drove quickly.

We arrived at the hospital and the general consensus was appendicitis. I have a high pain tolerance and because the appendix can calm down between bursts of venom, doctors were uncertain of the diagnosis. Just before they sent me home, one doctor called in another doctor who happened to be walking by. She was young, lovely and Asian. She palpated my lower right side. It was extremely uncomfortable. She turned to the other doctors and said in a very strong accent, "His appendik 'bout to burst. Take him upstair, now!"

The surgery was a success. The appendix did not burst, though I did get an infection that kept me in Kaiser's hands longer than planned. Adam came to visit me every day for five days. He was loving every minute. I remember hanging up the phone on him, sweetly, one evening because the Demerol was so much more fun. "I love you, honey, but this Demerol is something else."

He understood.

I forgot to mention the great sex in Mendocino. With marijuana and the waves breaking. Afterward, looking at our feet, giggling about how weird bodies are, head on top and then on the other end these things, these feet that are absolutely nothing like the head. All those ridiculous toes!

And the meals. The meals! The pork chops and the famous linguini with clam sauce and the Caesar with lime chicken. The meat loaf on the stove with the brown mushroom gravy he learned from my mother, the sausage risotto, the squash risotto, the turkey cutlets with lemon and capers, the couscous of all kinds, the ground turkey slop with stewed tomatoes, the tofu dish with the fried parmesan cheese over rice noodles, the bean soups with Swiss chard, the chicken soups with organic chickens, the London broil on the grill, the slow-cooked pulled pork and corn bread, the cheddar-with-parsley omelets, the waffles with unsalted butter and real maple syrup, the poached pears with crème fraiche, the delicate apple cake and the exploding taste sensation of the sweet and tart strawberry-rhubarb pies! Who the *fuck* is going to make me all of those things again? Who the hell else understands my horrible digestive system? That garlic makes me sick? That horseradish and shallots and mustard are just as bad? That I need to eat mountains of vegetables boiled into mush?

And our girl, our dog Louise, who followed me home one night. A Yorkie with benefits! A mutt is what I mean, who looked mostly terrier. We housetrained her intermittently and loved her for seven years and then one day we went to the vet together and held her while she died. More about her later, because we both never loved anything more.

Our dead cats. The ones we had to move outdoors and into a protected cat condo Adam had devised in a garage stall because I had become so allergic. Adam's resistance to moving the cats out of the house. The You-Don't-Care-About-Me fights! How I did not want to come back from a trip to Ireland with my father and brother because I knew I would have to face a partner in Los Angeles who would not budge on the pussy issue, who loved his cats more than he loved me, and how I called my friend Tim in New York on the phone at JFK while switching planes from Shannon, sobbing because I did not want to return to Los Angeles, ever. Tim told me to get on the plane, which I did, and because of some completely freakish tail wind that moved east to west, I landed at LAX in three and one-half hours. "It happens sometimes," a flight attendant said. I thought it must have been a sign or was at least something weird to remember. Then we did move the cats out to the garage cat condo and Adam did admit it was much better for me. He wrote a story about it that was very funny. In the closing paragraph he admitted he loved me more than the cats, which was pleasing.

His very sturdy body. His stamina. His adventurousness.

The four-way we had up in the Berkshires, just that one time, with the two fat guys—one guy a cousin of a friend of mine who was actually my girlfriend in the seventh grade, who ended up with another girlfriend of mine, Nola, from the eighth grade, as a lesbian couple—Oh, the Berkshires! Adam was the only one who was really able to maintain a full erection with the two big bears. I watched Adam, tall and lean, wrapped around the one hog of a man, not the cousin of my friend, but the cousin's boyfriend, the one with the slight brain damage from a car accident. Adam fucked him anally. I immediately thought of a slice of bacon wrapped around a scallop. Everyone eventually got off that night, but Adam got off the best. I was very impressed. We only ever saw those guys one other time and we did not do it again. It was so ridiculous the first time that a repeat was not necessary. We always referred to them as The Bad News Bears. Who would remember the night with The Bad News Bears? Laugh about it and remember how it *felt* to do something so outside what we usually did?

How I nursed him during his Hepatitis A while I was producing a play. His eyes were the color of spinach water. How he helped me put up the sets for that play once he got better.

How the day Louise, our lovely dog—here we go again—was diagnosed with inoperable terminal cancer and the producer of the theater where my play, *A Good Smoke*, was being performed called to tell me Meryl Streep was coming to see it that night—her son, Henry, my talented musician-actor friend, was in the play—I said to Adam that I just could not go, that I was too upset about my dying dog, and Adam, after feeding me a sad dinner said, "Get in that car and drive to the Valley, now."

And he was right. And I did. Which led to all sorts of career shenanigans like a monster-sized agency representing me, our moving to the studio in Queens, Meryl doing a reading of the play, and a Broadway option that never would have happened had Adam not pushed me into my white, dented 1992 Geo Prizm the night I learned my precious pooch was going to die and Meryl Streep was going to see my play, but ultimately did not end up getting me a production of the play anyway (at least it hasn't yet) even though I gave the entire cast grill pans as thank you gifts, even after The Talk of the Town piece in *The New Yorker* about the reading by the Streep-Gummer clan was published. The whole thing dropped dead after my intelligent, creative producers, who pushed hard for years, ultimately dropped out—Showbiz, baby—so maybe I should have just stayed home and cried over my girl pooch since success is never really guaranteed, anyway? I do not know. But what a night.

Guffman, as in *Waiting for*, actually showed up and Adam made sure I experienced the experience. He was practical. Above. All. Else.

The time I was having panic attacks at the best movie theater in America, the ArcLight in Hollywood, in the pre-show restaurant, because I had been on phase one of the South Beach Diet for too long—it had been weeks—and I lost thirty pounds too quickly so my metabolism and my mind were quite unstable and Adam tried to force a French dip sandwich down my throat while also telling me that he was afraid he was going to have to commit me. Commit me? For panic attacks? Really? This is not a good memory. I am going negative here.

I am going negative! They say you need to have someone who can be there for you when you are really down, especially when you get older. That is the most important thing in a long-term relationship. But hell, he was amazing during the appendicitis. Maybe he just can't do panic?

All his successes and failures that came in waves. All mine, which often crested while his fell and vice versa. His Golden Cassette for the *101 Dalmatians* read along. My *LA Weekly* Award for musical direction of a Steinbeck play. His emotional lunacy over being passed over for staffing season for sitcoms. My lunacy for getting older and not actually becoming a movie star, or anything, exactly, but a guy in his drawstring pants sitting at his computer typing up things that he always thought were interesting.

But I had friends. Good friends. And Adam. Always there.

Or the sex. The good sex. The bad sex. The hot Mendocino sex. Maintenance sex that when completed required the refrain, "That wasn't sex, that was mime," easy just-get-me-off sex, sex on high Sundays, sex in a gorgeous hotel room of a converted chateau outside of St. Remy, in Provence, that looked out onto swans in canals, sex in a Motel 6 at the Spokane airport, where we smuggled in Louise and had to keep her a secret and snuck her out for a walk at midnight as a grandma and her granddaughter were sneaking snacks from the vending machine at the bottom of the stairs while another guy was sneaking a cigarette out in the snow, everyone behaving illicitly, full of excitement—we would always have that.

The basic bottom nature of Adam and his not caring that I was not an 8 × 5, at least not to my face. The nipples, the ass, the sack, the shaft. All of it. His insistence as we got older that we both shower before sex (and he was right). How sex with anyone else, as the years wore on, felt a bit wrong and weird and lonely. Sex after a fight—but usually at least a day later, after the anger had cleared. Sex that sometimes sort of fell apart, everyone forgiving everyone. Peyronie's sex, that, with some effort, could happen. I had gotten so used to all those sexy ways.

The love. The hate with the love. The resented connection. The warm days when it was simply only about love. How I knew it was real love and how I was so grateful that it endured. How every day, every single day, we loved each other more and more and we felt it and we showed it.

But under the right circumstances, memories intact, I could still leave Adam. And maybe now was the time. Because when it's time, it's time.

I had to pee. I went to the bathroom and took out my penis and said to it—We're going to be fine, you and me.

I took a deep breath over the toilet and let my mind clear. My penis did the rest.

·15·

ACCEPTANCE

Hideous Monster

I wish I could say that I grew the balls to walk out or that there was another huge fight that really forced his hand or that Adam regressed and hit me or I hit him hard enough that it could end and then some prince walked through my door to tell me I was the most precious beast on earth and he would care for me in the nicest way, no matter what shape my penis was in. But there was something Adam and I quietly understood. We had reached the stage in our relationship where achieving escape velocity would basically require a trip to CERN, where upon arrival we would easily forget our purpose and fall into a bubbling vat of mixed Gruyere and Emmantaler, grinning from ear to ear that we had gotten so lucky. After my third Verapamil treatment in the second round of six, when I said to Adam, "You either stay committed to me, fully, forever, or I am out of here, I mean it" and received no response, I simply waited. Thinking. Obsessing. Taking inventory.

I repeated the request a few days later.

My anger had abated, but I wanted an answer with no caveats, codicils or holdbacks.

We were sitting across from each other, getting ready for one of his meals.

Adam, unprovoked, said, "Okay."

"Okay, what?"

"Okay, we shouldn't break up."

I did not believe him.

"It's going to end, isn't it?" I asked.

I reminded him of one of our favorite quotes from the Todd Solondz movie *Happiness*. The long marriage of a senior citizen couple in Florida comes to an end. Ben Gazzara announces to Louise Lasser that he is leaving her. Through her lonely, pathetic tears in a nondescript condo she screams, "Now I'll have to get another fucking facelift!"

We were both miserable. Adam's nasty father, who had never treated him well, was dead. I was not making a killer salary, not even maiming. We could not just pick up and go to Africa for safari whenever we wanted to, though we could go maybe once. We were, simply, disenchanted, disappointed and looking down the barrel of a waist-thickening, bald spot-making, body-jangling middle age. There are so many coming-of-age stories. And some of those are sexual coming-of-age stories, or maybe all of them are. An entire life can be a sexual coming of age with the right attitude. How can you get closer and closer to someone, sexually and intimately, as the decay sets in? Two Velveteen Rabbits with their ravaged button-eyed faces, worn fur and all that. There we were with what was left of us.

"So what you're telling me is, no matter what, no matter how difficult things get, you will no longer bring up breaking up with me?" I asked at our ravaged folding table.

"No."

"Never, ever again, because it makes me want to go completely crazy."

"I understand. I know."

Adam stood up. I stood up. Then he hugged me and looked into my eyes and he said, "I will never leave you."

And I believed him.

For my fourth treatment, on a perfect day in June, the mood was easygoing, jokey. There were a few nurses coming in and out. We all talked about our wacky mothers and how too much medicine was not a good thing.

"The doctors overprescribe," said John.

"Mothers too, especially if she works for a doctor and has a prescription pad—but that can also be very convenient," I added.

John told me how young kids, meaning guys in their twenties, come in with barely a bent penis and are completely freaked out. Some have to be sent for psychological counseling. John believes this is all because they watch too much porn. "They see these enormous straight penises and they don't understand why they don't have one. I explain to them that you have to think of these porn guys as actors, that most regular guys are six inches when erect. Plus, the larger penises never get as hard as the smaller ones. They never get up to a scale of ten in hardness. But six inchers, they will get up to a ten."

Nice. He finished. I left. It was a beautiful walk home in the park.

While he performed the fifth treatment, at the end of June, John talked about his early days working at the gay health clinic at NYU. I was in and out very quickly.

My final Verapamil treatment was on July 12, a little less than a year after I had met Dr. Hellman, seventeen months after I had discovered that my penis was bending and hurting. John talked about his upcoming trip to Hong Kong with his boyfriend. On my way out, in shorts, my wrapped-up penis was making an extra-large outward push. It was a very hot day. I was so happy to be finished.

Twelve treatments, three curvature assessments, with just one more assessment to go, Adam's father dying, too much wine, a kidnapping, an eighteen-year love relationship draining out into a lake of profound despair and depression, but saved at the last minute—I decided I had to simply accept however the hell this penis of mine was going to end up and where my psyche was going to end up with it. I would wear the AndroPenis for the rest of my life if that was what it took to keep my Peyronie's member *en pleine forme*. I became full and straight and thick the following five or six days after each of these last six treatments. But after the saline and Verapamil were absorbed, I went back to being curved upward and hourglass shaped, but less so each time. The improvement was obvious and definite, but the fear of reoccurrence did remain, and I did and still do have to stay on top of it.

I made a curvature assessment appointment, the last one, for October. I walked across the park thinking, again, about how when I was in my twenties I could walk into any public room, just look at someone, and they would have sex with me. But age will age you. Like Jackie Coogan's, my trajectory felt tragically ridiculous. Once the biggest film star in the United States, Jackie ended his career being cast on *The Addams Family* as Uncle Fester. Shortly after landing the gig, he was quoted as saying, "I used to be the most beautiful child in the world and now I'm a hideous monster!"

My final curvature assessment was on October 14, fifteen and a half months after my first visit with Dr. Hellman. My appointment was for 1:30 but I was not seen until 3:00. Angered, I calmed down when they finally brought me in. Regina entered with a needle, ready to plump up my penis for a curvature inspection. I said, "You know, nothing's really changed. Maybe we don't have to do this?"

"I'll get the doctor."

She returned with a red-faced Dr. Hellman. "Why didn't you cancel the appointment if you weren't going to do the curvature assessment?"

"I'm not against doing it, exactly. I just wanted to know if it's necessary. I am basically normal now. The only thing that really remains is this slight constriction ring, just below the center of my shaft. At times it loosens up. Especially if I am diligent with the AndroPenis. But then sometimes it gets worse. I'm curved a little, upward."

"Are you in a long-term relationship?"

"Eighteen years."

He said, "Well, if you were in your twenties looking for a boy or a girl, maybe we'd try something else."

He did not say right away what that something else was. But I figured he meant the Nesbit surgery.

He continued, "How is your psychology?"

"Fine." Whose is ever really exactly fine?

"Can you still have intercourse?"

I told him I certainly could, which was the total truth, something that I was not so much proud of as meekly relieved about.

"Is your erection stable?" Dr. Hellman asked.

"Yes."

"Are you still using the AndroPenis?"

"Yes. Should I keep adding half-centimeter pieces?"

"Yes, as long as you can."

"What about the vacuum device?"

"Five minutes a day."

Five minutes a day sounded useless to me. Did I hear him wrong? I stuck with ten. The appointment was drawing to an end. I did not undergo a curvature assessment. We only talked. I went on about my plaque and its size. Dr. Hellman said quickly, "You are a high-adrenaline type. You should only examine your penis when it is erect."

Apparently, the reputation of my adrenaline-rich blood exacerbating my penis problem was considered to be in full, unending force—and wrong. Let him be cranky. I was glad this was over. Dr. Hellman wanted to bring this to a conclusion. "You are not a candidate for surgery. It takes three hours to separate the nerves from the scar tissue and then you can have erection problems in addition to sensation problems."

For one constriction ring and a tiny amount of upward bending, I would not have any kind of surgery, not that he was offering. I now just had to make the unacceptable acceptable: a less-than-perfect penis as my penis.

The last thing Dr. Hellman told me was that clinical trials had been completed with collagenase and that the drug had gone to the FDA for approval. "In the early part of next year it should be passed."

"Will you call me when it's available?"

"There are too many, hundreds of men, to call. There will most likely be collagenase clinics set up all over town once this happens."

This sounded grandiose to me. I made a note to look it up online, to see if I could get the treatments sooner, in Europe or South America—but only because I am a perfectionist and wanted my penis to be as wonderful as it had been almost two years ago. I would be happy to rid myself of this slightly deforming ring and the small upward tilt, even though I am perfectly capable of being erect, full of pleasure, somewhat bent but not broken.

I met Mr. Rubble, the one from Rockefeller Center, one last time. He no longer needed anything from me. Since he was a careerist, time was of the essence. He had taken his own path, gotten what he needed from our first two encounters, so instead of meeting at my place he asked if I would meet him at The Rock so we could walk together and have more time to talk. We did end up at my apartment. It was clear to me, from watching other careerists in other arenas who had gotten what they needed and had moved on, that these were going to be our last moments together. He talked faster than ever and was entirely distant, outside his body. Poor thing. Vulnerability abounding. I would have liked to hold him like a baby.

As we walked I asked, "What happened with the collagenase treatment?"

"It didn't do anything. It was a waste of time. There was no improvement."

"Do you think they will set up collagenase treatment centers everywhere? Probably not, right?"

"I don't know."

We arrived at my apartment. We settled onto the solid brown sofa. I brought over tea.

"Are you going to go to Chicago?" I asked.

"I went."

"What? What happened?"

"I went to the best Nesbit procedure surgeon in the country. My penis is straightened but it's still not right."

We showed each other pictures of our penises. Befores and afters. It looked like he had not been given a whole lot to start with in comparison, making my average thumper look like a zeppelin. Visually, penis pictures are difficult to gauge unless there is a beer can nearby. No matter his size, Mr. Rubble was a much more aggressive person than I will ever be, so maybe he used his penis like it was a nine-inch love club.

"Is that what you had to start with?" he asked about my before picture.

"Yes." I was proud. It was a nice picture. But a close-up, so it was a bit of a lie.

"That's pretty good," his eyes lighting up with a bit of want.

He had penis size shame much more than I did. We men. No wonder, all these wars.

Mr. Rubble went on, "My erections before the surgery weren't too strong, and after they weren't any better. I use Cialis. I'll continue with those."

"They give me headaches. And strange feelings, like I'm going to faint. And acid reflux," I said.

"Not me. I'm mostly concerned for my boyfriend. He's young. For me, I'm almost fifty years old. I had a good run."

Mr. Rubble grew calm with his cup of tea. I could not imagine being that sanguine about the end of ready pleasure. I did not think he was, actually. He was running hard and fast away from the emotional pain of the situation. I was kind and soft toward him. His business soul did not find my softness compelling, or something he should give a lot of attention to. He left my apartment. I never saw him again.

·16·

THE NATURE OF OUR NATURE

Animal Husbandry

I have often been accused by Adam of behaving as if I am terrified that bad things are never going to get better. He is correct. I must have learned this from a lifetime of severe cyclical allergies taking me down every spring and fall. The bee sting that put me into a coma when I was four. The nonstop attacks by peers because I could not throw a ball or did not want to beat people up. Anxiety in college about my sexuality and career choices and drug use. Parents that assured me that life only got worse and more difficult, so I better make a lot of money. My acceptance of the forever bad was good practice. Some things are just baleful and diminishing. Sad and true. Like Peyronie's disease.

I have been almost fully cured so it is not terrible, but it may and probably will always be noticeable. Though improved, it probably will not go away entirely. But at least it isn't cancer. My penis is bent slightly upward now, like many penises are naturally. It still has a slight constriction ring. It has a slightly smaller circumference. It is harder when erect. It is a lesser-sized penis but, magically, with slightly stronger erections. Summation: during an erection, my penis feels tighter, it is more constricted in the middle, it is curved slightly upward, and it simply looks a little smaller than it used to. My penis is straight enough so the ejaculate exits. Whereas I once had to be careful how I stood when urinating if I was at all erect, now I can simply pee.

Adam did not talk about breaking up any longer. When he said he would never talk about breaking up again, I waited. I waited for him to shimmy back to wanting to take off. He had been known to perform that sparkly move. I waited for weeks for him to turn to me and say, "If you don't have a job within three months, we are finished." But he did not. I do not think it was a poor choice for me to believe that he would not stay with me. I was girding myself for the possible transition to becoming single. I did ramp up the job hunt, but I was not convinced that any money I brought home would assuage his disappointment with me. He was not the only one in our relationship who was disappointed. I often calculated his assets, emotional, financial and otherwise, and wanted him gone. There had been plenty of times, especially in the early years of our relationship, when each of us was ready to walk out the fucking door. But these emotional flare-ups had flared down. I always say to humans struggling in a new relationship—The first ten years are the hardest.

Our sex life was back on track. I was inserting and Adam was enjoying my smaller but harder penis. I had to use a dildo to loosen him up so I could get inside with less trouble and less pained irritation to my penis. Buckets of lubrication, or what we have always called *hiney sauce*, were and are essential.

Adam still wanted me to get a job. I still wanted him to be more affectionate. We did both of these things. He touched me more. I taught at a university and jumped into some other freelance things.

Adam's father's body was dissected at a medical school in Washington State and whatever was left of the corpse was burned, the ashes sent to Adam's mother. This transition into our full-blown middle years, together, was revocable, but we did not revoke it.

On our eighteenth anniversary, Adam and I got married. Bent

on one ironic knee in front of Adam sitting on our sturdy sofa, I proposed July 24, the evening it became legal in New York State, two months after Adam had wanted to dump me for being unemployed but resisted because I was penis-challenged. We were both so happy. It felt wildly romantic, to finally be included with all the straight people in the legal department. We had been married once before, six years prior, in Multnomah County in Oregon, in Portland. A March ski trip was turned into a wedding weekend because of the timing. For geographical expedience, it took place in Pioneer Square, a red brick public space. We stood in front of a tub of yellow daffodils with Nordstrom and Banana Republic lurking behind us. A ragtag bunch of Adam's family attended. Soon after, the state of Oregon revoked all the marriage licenses. We were very cynical about marriage. California had its Proposition H8 that choked the fairness of the land just before we left Los Angeles. All we had in California was a domestic partnership, signed and notarized at a Mail Boxes Etc. in Larchmont Village, then sent off to Sacramento.

I was afraid I might have made the wrong decision, having forgiven Adam for wanting to break up with me at such a vulnerable time in my life and then offering to marry him. But then, it is always a good time to forgive someone, especially with the government on your side, and getting married was especially heartwarming in New York, the state where I was born.

Our wedding was witnessed by my sister and her spouse and our close friends, David and Cynthia, the college couple who, from the East Coast, made sure the dinner where we were introduced happened at Susan's on the West Coast. It was a beautiful day, our wedding day (the wedding that actually took), on October 20, our anniversary and my Aunt Rita's birthday. She had died by then. We did not make love on our wedding night. We were exhausted. But we did go out to eat at a noisy restaurant in Chelsea. I had sea bass.

Relationship problems never fully go away. Adam did agree to stay committed, though people say things they may not mean, even when they are married. But being married, for both of us, truly feels like a cementer. Something changed. For better or for worse—we had seen so much of better and worse—we were well-rehearsed for the days ahead. Adam still resents me, a little, for not having a job commensurate with my abilities. I am resentful, some, because affection is doled out in planned increments: a short backrub every weekday, some sex on Sundays. I have heard other marriages have it worse. Our most positive bond is that we enjoy each other's company. There is a lot of joking. Word play. We like to travel and enjoy some of the same television shows. We are very used to each other. And dammit, I still like to fuck him. And lucky for me, he is still very attractive and lets me climb on. His libido is decreasing, or his sexual interest in me has waned, or both. I am in a new surge of excitement about sex because my penis is working and the pain has disappeared.

My penis continues to get better, and it's not only in my mind but can be seen in the few pictures I took during the struggle. Erect, it still has the mild mid-constriction ring and the small upward curve, but it has completely stabilized and it does not get worse. Most of my adulthood, it was close to perpendicular to my body when erect. In some ways, this new direction is better. My penis is about a quarter inch shorter. This is too bad but not the end of the world. The constriction ring is almost unnoticeable on the right side. It is noticeable across the top, not as an indent but more as the torque that pulls my penis closer up toward my body. There is a small, clear indent on the left, as if a mouse had taken a small bite out of that side, but there are days when that mouse bite completely disappears. After the treatments were finished, my penis was slightly less thick above the ring than below, but over time that dissipated and now my whole penis is the same thickness except for the bit of mid-constriction. Perhaps it is this small ring that makes my erections harder than they used to be before all this began. A Darwinian advantage for middle-aged men, this Peyronie's disease? I am optimistic that one day the constricting tissue, which I always feel when erect, will loosen up or that the FDA will approve collagenase and it will work. However, I met a man online, on a Peyronie's website, who was in trial experiments for the collagenase and said it truly did nothing, as Mr. Rubble said.

I have no idea if it was the treatments that worked or if time just took care of everything. There was no control "me." I had a great sense that the AndroPenis did a lot for my penis. Anything that helps stretch scar tissue and brings more blood into the penis is helpful. When inside the body, blood does good things. I do believe the Verapamil treatments helped me.

I had an appointment to make a final call to Dr. Hellman to tell him how things were going. I did wonder if Dr. Hellman's penis was okay. I never asked. I rightly realized in my early forties that I was not my teeth and hair. Now, I've added my penis to that list. And eventually I will check off my entire body.

I called Dr. Hellman. I told him I was well and my mind was clear.

"I'm happy you're not perseverating. This is important." He then added, "Studies with collagenase have proven not so much that it works, but that men feel better that they are doing it."

I had nothing to say to that. I asked, "What should I do now?"

"Do two hours per day of traction with the AndroPenis and two or one fifteen-minute vacuum pumps per day. Do not go up and down. Bring it up and leave it up for fifteen minutes. If in three months you see improvement with the constricting ring, continue. If not, then stop. Repeat the self-reassessment every three months."

"Sounds good."

Then, "In a few months, I am going to do a DNA study—one thousand men with Peyronie's. One thousand without. And among the Peyronie's, treated and untreated, who got better. Would you come in and give sputum?"

"Well sure!"

I was a lucky one. As I have mentioned, some guys, about fifteen to twenty percent, get worse during the treatment. The scariest thing of all was I did not know if I was going to be one of those guys. I got better. I won. And now my prize was being asked to give sputum. This would be my gift to Dr. Hellman, the man who may have cured me of my Peyronie's disease or maybe just convinced me to join the group of men who agreed to have needles stabbed into their penises on a regular basis. But I have been through worse. And I survived how I could.

When I grew up, gay and all, homosexuality was so frowned upon and I was so depressed about it I wanted to fuck in retaliation. You press a person enough against themselves, they will become even more that thing. I was pushed into isolation. I was one of those children who begged for magic. I would say, "God, make me magic. Make me able to fly. Disappear. Let me be able to do all sorts of things that others cannot do. And I won't tell anybody about it." That would be our deal. And instead of feeling like a pariah, I would feel special.

This was my desire to separate, for good, from the forces around me and at the same time to feel like I had more power than everyone else. This is nothing new for children who are alone or vulnerable. But God, that abstract gift-giver, never signed on, so I had to look for other ways out. Music was fun but eventually became something I was going to have to get very serious about if I wanted to become a professional. It was too solitary and it ultimately meant performing in bars and clubs, something I did not want to do. Academia, theater, they sustained me, but they were always work. Writing took over later.

More than anything else, the transcendence really came from sex. It was freedom and I wanted to pursue that freedom. I wanted to use my dick any way I liked at any time. If I wanted to get close, there I was. If not, there I wasn't, but my body still was. This was a problem, of course, for obvious reasons. You can end up feeling lonely. However, I do now have this husband, and because of my culturally Catholic upbringing, with parents who were also not exactly suited to each other but saw it through anyway, I cannot imagine this arrangement ending. Adam and I understand that we are each independent, even sexually independent if necessary. Since his libido has decreased and I would like to continue the sex party, he tells me, "Do what you want. I understand." But at this point, it is an easier arrangement to spend time with these penises we have at home.

When I was in elementary school, through the fifth grade, we lived in a large white high ranch house in a development in Spring Valley, New York, sandwiched between Hillcrest and Monsey. Most of the families were transplants from the lower-middle-class outer boroughs. Brooklyn, back when it was Brooklyn. Queens. The Bronx. My parents were from Yonkers. Spring Valley was not romantic. It was full of tough Italianate kids—at least the ones who were in charge of the neighborhood were tough. The Jewish kids were sweeter, but they mostly stayed indoors, away from the aggression. I stayed inside because I did not like noise, horseplay, games that required hitting a ball or hitting each other, but mostly because I liked to play music and make things.

When I was nine years old I started drawing funny pictures, mostly having to do with Snoopy on his doghouse. Then one day I started drawing penises, with testicles. At first, I drew them so the penis was actually hanging off the sack of balls. I felt like all you needed was to get them all on the page, and then you had them and so you had a rendition that worked. Those pictures looked like a cucumber hanging off a grapefruit. They got me very excited and after I made a few, comparing the bigger ones to the smaller ones, the meatier to the leaner, I would crumple them all up and throw them out so no one would know what I was up to.

One day, I realized I was not really drawing things correctly. The pictures were not ringing true. I walked across the indoor-outdoor carpet tiles, mostly deep red, with some royal blue ones diagonally designed in, to the bathroom and looked at my own equipment and realized the scrotum and the penis were pretty much all attached to the body at the same spot and that the penis hung in front. This meant I had to draw the balls first, erase a section at the bottom of the scrotum, and then draw in the good penis, connected at top but hanging past the ball sack. These got me even more excited, not only because they looked more like the real thing, but also because I actually gave myself the first lesson of art: express, honestly and clearly, what you see.

I continued to draw penises during all of elementary school and then added hair in the junior high years. I would make them as big as possible. I would then put glasses on them, with eyeballs, the penis as the nose, and cross them out or rip them up. It was something to do that gave me my own place to be, separate from everyone else. It was pleasurable and secretive. This led to so much secret sexual pleasure later on and I was happy to enjoy that. And though there are so many stories involving my pleasure, from the sand dunes of Jones Beach to hotel rooms in Manhattan, in Parisian bar bathrooms with multiple suitors down to a lakeside utility hut in Zurich that I simply intuited was a fellatio barn, there is nothing more tawdry than sex on a bus or, even worse, at a bus station. When sex talks come up, my close friends in Los Angeles, buzzed at a party, will often ask, while grinning, getting ready to laugh, "Tell us the one again about the Port Authority," and I do.

My parents moved to Ramsey, New Jersey when I was a sophomore in college, the worst year of my life with the drugs, the harsh reality of my sexuality, anxiety and all. While my mother would pant on the phone about all their money running out because I was at an expensive college during a recession, I would come home to find her in a new fur coat or two, and then this surprising move to an upper-middle-class neighborhood, complete with a stone clubhouse brought over from England—they disassembled it on the east side of the Atlantic, numbered the stones and reassembled the thing in New Jersey—a full golf course, lakes and paddle tennis.

This was not how I was raised, so when my parents would take us to eat at the fake English clubroom and simply sign for dinner when the check came, I was annoyed, proud and confused. These corporate people, working at IBM and points beyond, were friendly but behaved suspiciously. They slapped each other on the back while recounting the last holes of their golf games. Lots of middle-aged drinking going on. It was Reagan time. It was oppressive. I was surly, with my huge hair flying in every direction. My parents wanted to show me off as their college kid who was headed for medical school. I wanted to get the hell out of there. I hated these shut-down clubby folks and wanted nothing to do with them. I was jealous of their plumy lives and sickened by their insular concerns. Be gone bad white zombies!

But it was not without its pleasures. If you were to take the bus from Ramsey, New Jersey to the Port Authority Bus Terminal in New York City and sit toward the back, there was usually a husband or two from the area who was happy to jerk you off as you hurtled down Route 17. That was fun. But what about that guy with the tan briefcase, that one day? He was sitting next to me but there were too many people around. What were we to do?

In a situation like that, you start rubbing your hand against his thigh and his against yours. Maybe get a hand under and grab a little ass. Eventually, the both of you are so bonered up it dawns on you, long before you get to Lincoln's old tunnel, that as soon as this bus pulls in, you are going to have to find a place to blow one out. I would like to say rub one out, but they didn't say that then.

The bus pulled into Port Authority. We got off. He said, "Follow me." We went to a bathroom. Nah. Not enough privacy. We went to another bathroom. The inn was full. He gave me a look, knowing exactly what to do.

"Come on."

With his curly thinning hair, looking much like a perm but not, and with great purpose, he led me out to another bus platform and we turned a corner to where there were some parked busses, busses that he must have known, from experience, sat there in the morning, unused. We got between two busses. He started to blow me. Then he turned around in his floppy spring suit the color of earthworms in spring puddles, dropped his poly trousers, put one hand on his one knee for support and expected to be plowed in his ass. I plowed.

The whole time I was banging against him, my young thick penis fully inserted into his midlife corporate ass, my pubic hair brushing up against his crack, he held his briefcase in his other hand. It swung back and forth in time to the fucking. I was young and horny enough not to be turned off by his briefcase swinging to the rhythm of my thrusts, but I did remember a distracting physics equation that measured the period of a pendulum—the square root of (length dived by acceleration due to gravity) multiplied by a constant. I shot on his back. He pulled up his pants. He said thanks and goodbye and went off to work with his ugly hair and clunky briefcase. I thought—He's going to be so dirty all day long.

I knew I was going to be late for school and miss my first class. This was acting school. Two years at The Neighborhood Playhouse with teachers both supportive and abusive, often alternating within the same personality. I walked over to the East Fifties, leisurely, went to the basement where we had lockers and showers, and cleaned up. A future famous actor, Dylan McDermott, was a year ahead of me. He was called Mark back then. He had just gotten out of dance class and changed in front of me. He loved to change in front of people. His body was incredible—tight, long, lean and hung like you want it. It was my final treat for that bus terminal sex morning and then, all scrubbed down, I went off to class as if nothing had ever happened.

I am less sexually confident now than I was as a young acting student in New York escaping the fake English countryside of Bergen County, New Jersey to have sex on a platform of the world's largest bus depot. I do prefer having sex with my husband to having sex with strangers. Adam and I know what works for each other. Strangers either go too fast, too slow, too soft or too hard. When you communicate to a stranger, "More this, less this, slow down, feel it, slow down," they often get annoyed. They do not show it, but they also will not necessarily do what you ask. They are there to do whatever the hell they want for their own pleasure.

This is the problem with men. Not all. But most. They want the pleasure they want. If they cannot have it how they want it at home, they go on a hunt. If the hunt does not yield the exact desired result, they continue to adjust their prey into giving what is wanted. This truly is what men will do. French men accept this without guilt. The women have responded in kind. If this goes against the cultural trope that monogamy is better, and I romantically do believe it is, it cannot be helped. If there is any sense of decency to this Peyronie's disease story, it is that at least I am being honest. And honesty is the best police? No, policy.

I continue to admit what I want to Adam and others, and I continue to accept what shape my penis is actually in. I want my husband, but I also have a pleasure stick and I want to use it as much as possible. Men are animals. We cannot resist. No matter what shape our dicks are in. Mine is not as pretty as it once was, but there is no pain, just pleasure. It looks like a penis, it feels like a penis, so it must be a penis.

I could say I will only ever again have sex with my husband, the man who did not leave me, but I know when he is not willing and I get insecure on the sexual highway of life, I will want to take my penis out for a test drive. This may seem immature, a leftover response to handling stress and ego amplification, my escape hatch, but perhaps not. Maybe it is the best use of adult choice.

I have used my penis like a drug, the act of trawling becoming a speedball followed by a tranquilizer. I have used it to make myself feel better than what I am after a boring day or a career disappointment. Peyronie's disease (again, a condition, not a disease) has punished me for overusing my penis or I have been visited upon by a random misfortune. I will never know. The neurotic in me feels guilty. The scientist in me does not have a control to compare with. If only I had tied up an identical twin somewhere, I could maybe get to the bottom of this.

I am lucky, or lazy, that I have this husband, this imperfect, retreating husband who has worked hard to be more present, who loves when I fuck him and who is much more consistent loving me than I want to admit. Because like all men, I really do want to get close, but it's complicated. Because like a lot of curious, alive men, I want to ride the rails, get drunk, smoke everything, sing songs with my guitar under the moonlight and fuck whatever grabs my fancy. This railroad action always starts exciting but usually leaves me sad and invisible. Except for the rare occasion when it feels like the exact thing I needed on a Wednesday, I much more look forward to my husband for a Sunday afternoon ride.

We retain a Don't-Ask-Don't-Tell marriage. Adam is surprised that he is not as enthused about sex as he used to be. He also has less free time. He works. I do my best to keep the pleasure at home. Every day, it becomes clearer that I am better off setting my sights on Adam, always on Adam. But when he disappoints me, when I get angry, when the whole thing feels impossible, I just want to run away and join the circus. But as what? The middle-aged, medium-height, averagely-attractive, slightly-imperfect-penis man? You never know. There might be a slot.

My penis, though a joy stick that works in many situations, ultimately gives me greater pleasure if I see that it gives my husband greater pleasure. I get closer to him. And he really likes it. Joy is shared. Thanks to Dr. Hellman, the AndroPenis, the vacuum device, the Verapamil treatments, my homosexuality making me over-identified with my penis, which pushed me to go in early to be observed, and my willingness to prevail, my penis is 94% of what it once was. It functions. But like most men over forty-five, I am not the stud I used to be. Korean red ginseng helps, taken an hour before sex. A cock ring for extra support, too, when I'm tired. Lessen the booze, increase the water. And a good night's sleep. But some days are simply better than others.

My goal was to save my penis, to keep it as close to its original glory as possible. This was achieved, mostly. My penis works. I still like it. But let's face it, how many erections do I have left in me? Nine-hundred more strong ones, with someone around to see them if I am lucky? I will be better off, happier and calmer, if I give my husband about seven hundred and fifty of those. I probably should give him even more. Maybe I have a thousand, even, to share? I do not know. I do know my sexual market value has been diminished by age, Peyronie's disease, those hundreds of pork chops I've eaten since the late 1960s and my certain natural drop in testosterone.

Delusional am I to believe I am attractive enough or energetic enough to continue carrying on in any wild, loose way with all the godlike Ganymedes who, really, long ago moved on to younger, sexier, harder fare. I have a husband who will still have me in spite of everything, and we both prefer to have sex with each other over anyone else. My penis is dangerous now, a survivor of some weird negative energy, which actually adds to its magic. Our sex life is lovely and we basically get what we need. I still sometimes pine for more affection and Adam still tells me it would not bother him at all if I were to find it elsewhere. I do, rarely, but I always return home. Part of affection that is irreplaceable is the intimate knowledge of another person. We are amazed that after all these years we still have sex together and it is still exciting. Adam and I still marvel at our erections and what they can do. Wait, I think I might be getting one right now. False alarm. Just a temporary rise of blood and a thickening. Even that felt really good.

·17·

WRAPPING IT UP

Members Only

There are books and websites that promote many different treatments, procedures and supplements for Peyronie's disease. I have only included what methods I pursued and what improvements I achieved. Many touted supplements and programs have been proven to be ineffective, dangerous or simply a waste of time. Gentle stretching, manipulation of scar tissue and increased blood flow to the penis are common denominators in all publications, sites and studies. These are good options to consider under the supervision of a physician. You will make your own choices for how to proceed, steadily and safely, with the repair of your bending penis. Remember, I am one person who went on one journey. I enjoy sex and I am scientifically minded so I was very motivated to heal my penis and kept my mind as clear as possible in order to gather evidence during a very emotional time. But again, I am one person with one particular penis. I have only included what actually worked for me. Information changes. Do not consider me the official source. I am obviously fallible and clearly human, and humans are tricky mammals to deal with. My case of Peyronie's disease was moderate, but debilitating enough to me sexually and emotionally that I felt compelled to help others.

You are an individual and your experience will be unique. When visiting Peyronie's sites online where men post their opinions, keep in mind these suffering men are in various states of dealing with their Peyronie's disease. There is ongoing research, but still, no one knows exactly what causes Peyronie's disease and there is no complete cure unless you are one of the lucky ones whose Peyronie's disease fully disappears as mysteriously as it arrived. Be wary of charlatans who want to sell you crazy things that can be dangerous or at the least useless and expensive. Also, some men with Peyronie's disease who chat online may proffer conspiracy theories about their affliction and trash talk all sorts of treatments. They would love to have you join them on their planet called I Am Miserable and I Want Company!

Though I do get emotional and feel abandoned during stress, that is my problem. You may be nothing like this and I applaud you. On the other hand, you may grow much unhappier than I did if your penis starts acting up, in which case, in addition to seeking physical treatment, I suggest psychotherapy, meditation and trips to favorite places. Taking action is essential. I like to solve problems and I like to be calm and happy. I have arrived at an acceptable place with my penis and with my closest loved one. I wish you the same.

You will have your hopeless, angry, sad and frustrating days. Try to remain positive. No one ever died from Peyronie's disease.

ACKNOWLEDGEMENTS

To my body and to my mind, thank you for hanging in there, doing the best that you can do. My hearty gratitude to Naomi Rosenblatt and Heliotrope Books for your bravery and your commitment to taking literary risks and the creativity you use to bring books into the world. To my kind, intelligent agent, Anne Edelstein, I find myself feeling warm, grateful and even bashful. Thank you. It has been a great fortune to have Louise Crawford and Linda Quigley, my game and energetic publicists. They turned a daunting process into a smart celebration. Without Lisa Dierbeck, my friend and champion, I would not have known where to start. Thank you. To Marian Fontana, my buddy and cheerleader, I lovingly appreciate your insistence that I put my full humanity on the page. Thanks, Blair Fell, for zeroing in on trouble spots. Thank you Moss Turpan, for your fine edit, and to the folks at *Epiphany*, Willard Cook, Odette Heideman and Elizabeth England, for that literary family feel. I have great appreciation for Christopher X. Shade at *Cagibi* and Jotham Burrello at Yale Writers' Workshop for their peerless understanding of story and language in all works. Chip Kidd gives visual pleasure to everyone. And now this. Thank you. I appreciate my many creative friends and family on both coasts, hugging the Great Lakes and riding the high deserts who advised me and supported this work, Carla Barnett, Jaime Lubin, Billy Frolick, Georgia Clark, Jeffrey Sugerman, Sarah Schultz, John Bianchi, Kathleen Vance, Wayne Hoffman, Kim Merrill, Vibeke Weiland, Joseph Weiland, Vanessa McGrady, Kent Shell, Aaron Zimmerman, and the Cummings, Lynch and Waring clans, you are all so generous. And to my husband, Adam Waring, thank you for the love, the adventures, the humor, the pleasure, the music and the clam sauce.

ABOUT THE AUTHOR

Don Cummings is an author and playwright. He has been published in *Cagibi, Epiphany, The Coachella Review* and *Post Road Magazine*, and often performs at Comedy Central's Sit 'n Spin and other storytelling events. His plays have been developed and produced on both coasts. He lives in Los Angeles with his writer/musician husband, Adam Waring. **doncummings.net.**

CPSIA information can be obtained
at www.ICGtesting.com
Printed in the USA
FSHW022043030419
56954FS